HANS CHRISTIAN ANDERSEN

Fairy Tale Author

Hans Christian Andersen:

ILLUSTRATED BY JOHN GRETZER

4465

Fairy Tale Author

SHANNON GARST

HOUGHTON MIFFLIN COMPANY · BOSTON

NEW YORK · ATLANTA · GENEVA, ILL. · DALLAS · PALO ALTO

Contents

Copyright © 1965 by Houghton Mifflin Company. All rights reserved including the right to reproduce this book or parts thereof in any form. Printed in the U.S.A.

Library of Congress Catalog Card No. 65-10520

CHAPTER 1

Boyhood Home

Hans Christian Andersen was born in Odense, Denmark, on April 2, 1805. Near the end of his life he wrote, "Rich and serenely happy, my life is a beautiful fairy tale."

And fairy tale it was, but not because of any riches his parents owned, for they were very poor. His father, Hans Andersen, was a shoemaker, but his son had to wear wooden shoes, for there was not enough money to pay for the leather for boots. His mother was a washerwoman.

One of Hans Christian's early memories was of standing beside his father's bench watching him work on a pair of dancing shoes. The soles were of the finest leather he had in his shop. The tops were of red silk.

Father took the last stitches and held up the shoes for his son and wife to admire.

"They are beautiful!" Hans Christian cried, clapping his hands. "The lady on the farm will like them. They will make her feet want to dance. You are sure to get the job as shoemaker for the people in her big house."

"Oh, I hope so," said Anne Marie, his mother. "I would love to live in the country — to have a cow — to plant vegetable and flower gardens — to sit under a tree beside a stream."

It sounded like a dream of heaven to Hans Christian.

Father wrapped the red slippers in a clean handkerchief and set out to walk to the fine country home.

While he waited for Father to come back, Hans Christian climbed the ladder to the roof, where Mother had a tiny garden of parsley and chives in a box. He sat down at the edge of the roof and let his long legs dangle. He watched the clouds make different shapes and dreamed of living in the country where they

would have a little house of their own instead of one room on which they had to pay rent.

Getting tired of watching the clouds, he climbed down into the small room which was both shop and home. He drew back the curtains of his toy theater and started playing with it. Father had made it from a box. Hans Christian had carved the small wooden figures that were his actors and had made the clothes himself from bits of cloth Mother and the neighbors had given him.

Mother was making stew for supper. She knew that her husband would be hungry from his long walk. The smell of boiling meat and vegetables made the boy's mouth water. Yet Mother would not let him eat until Father came home.

It was late when he got there, and his face was not happy as they had thought it would be. Instead it was lined with tiredness, and his eyes were angry.

"Didn't the lady like the slippers? Didn't you get the job?" Hans Christian cried.

"She did not even try them on," Father replied. "She said I had spoiled her silk. Then I told her that I would also spoil my fine leather, and I took out my knife and cut it into strips."

"You are tired," Mother said kindly as she served the stew. "You will feel better when you have eaten. We have to take disappointments as they happen."

She spoke bravely, but Hans Christian saw her quickly wipe the tears from her eyes. His own heart felt like lead.

Father pushed his plate away. "I'm not hungry," he said.

He folded his arms on the table, and his shoulders slumped. "I have a good mind," he said. "But I didn't have enough schooling to make something of myself. My parents apprenticed me to a shoemaker when I was ten. I shall have to go on making shoes all my life."

He sighed and then went on, "Anne Marie, our son must never be forced into any trade. We must allow him to be whatever he wants to be."

"Then I shall be an actor!" Hans Christian cried. He had been stage-struck ever since his grandmother, whom he dearly loved, had taken him to see a play. They sat in the highest balcony, and the figures on the stage were tiny, but the play brought a glow to his heart that he would never forget. The next day he coaxed Father to make the little stage for him, and the boy spent hours carving his little actors and making up plays for them to act out.

Hans Christian knew that he was a homely boy. He had long arms and legs and large hands and feet. His nose was too big and his blue eyes too small and close together. When he danced, as he often did for amusement, it was all that Father could do to keep from laughing. The boy was as awkward as a scarecrow.

Neither Hans Christian nor his parents had many friends, for there was a shadow over the family. Hans Christian's grandfather was insane. The old man was harmless enough to be allowed to wander about town while Grandma worked, but Hans Christian was ashamed of him.

The shoemaker and his son were good friends. The man read aloud by the hour to the wide-eyed boy who never tired of hearing the stories from *Arabian Nights* and the plays of the Danish writer Holberg.

On Sundays during the summer Father took Hans Christian to the woods. While the man lay resting, the boy played and watched the birds and animals.

He was always glad to return to the little room that was home to him. It was a poor and tiny place, but so filled with love that it always seemed to put warm arms about him when he came back to it. Mother kept it spick-and-span. The floor and furniture shone with cleanliness and the white curtains at the windows were crisp.

Later he described the room in his writings:

Our one little room had nearly all the space filled up with the shoemaker's bench, the bed, and the folding cot on which I slept. The walls were covered with pictures and over the workbench was a cupboard containing books and songs; the little kitchen had a row of shining pewter plates, and the small place seemed big and rich to me.

The door itself with landscape paintings on the panels was as much to me then as a whole art gallery.

He would later use that room often as a setting for his fairy tales. Always before he went to sleep, he stared at the paintings on the door. They gave him pleasant dreams. Some day he would put those landscapes into his story of "Ole Lukoie, the Dustman," who brought dreams to sleeping children:

Ole Lukoie touched the picture with his wand, and the birds in it began to sing, the branches of the trees moved and the clouds scudded along; you could see their shadows passing over the landscape.

13

Now Ole Lukoie lifted little Hialmar up close to the frame, and Hialmar put his leg right into the picture among the long grass, and there he stood; the sun shone down upon him through the branches of the trees. He ran to the water and got into a little boat which lay there; it was painted red and white, and the sails shone like silver.

. . . .

That was a sailing trip indeed! Now the woods were thick and dark, now they were like beautiful gardens full of sunshine and flowers, and among them were castles of glass and marble. Princesses stood upon the balconies, and they were all little girls whom Hialmar knew and used to play with.

They stretched out their hands, each one holding the most beautiful sugar pig which any cakewoman could sell.

Grandma, the mother of Hans Christian's father, came to the house every day to see her beloved grandson. She had kind blue eyes, pink skin, and silvery hair. She had come from a good home, but her parents had lost their money and become poor. Now she worked taking care of the garden of the Odense Old Folks Home.

Every Sunday evening she brought flowers from the garden.

"They are mine! Mine!" Hans Christian would cry. He would take them and arrange them with real skill in a blue vase.

When he was six, Mother entered him in an A B C school run by an old woman.

Hans Christian's mother said to the teacher, "Do not hit my boy. I do not want him struck."

Here he learned the alphabet, how to read, and how to spell a little. The teacher sat on a throne-like chair under the clock which opened upon every hour to let out a little cuckoo bird to tell the time.

Hans Christian was too shy to play with the other boys. At recess he stayed in the schoolroom looking at the pictures in books.

He was very much afraid of his grandfather, who roamed the streets with a basket on his arm. In it he carried the strange figures he had carved from wood — men with animals' heads and animals with wings. These he gave away to children he met.

One day on his way home from school Hans Christian saw a gang of boys chasing his grandfather, crying out, "Crazy man! Crazy man!"

Hans Christian hid, trembling, under some stairs until long after the shouting had died away.

The next day the teacher struck him over the knuckles with a ruler for not paying attention.

"My mother said you were not to hit me," he said. He picked up his books and went home.

"I'll not go back to that school," he told Father.

He went to the stream which flowed through the town. There his mother stood, up to her knees in the water, rubbing clothes on a rock.

"I quit school," Hans Christian told her. "The teacher hit me."

Mother straightened up. "You do not have to go back. Tomorrow I will take you to another school."

CHAPTER 2

The First Poem

Hans Christian's mother next took him to Mr. Carsten's school for boys. There was also one girl in the school. She and Hans became friends.

"I am here to learn arithmetic," she told him. "Then I shall become a dairymaid in some great manor."

"Then you can come to work at my castle when I become a nobleman," he said.

"But you are only a poor boy." She laughed.

One day he drew a picture of a castle and showed it to her. "I am really a child of high birth," he told her. "The angels of God come down and speak to me."

He had expected to impress her, but she stared at him for a moment, then turned to the boy beside her and he heard her say, "He is weak in the head like his grandfather."

From that time on, he paid no more attention to her nor she to him. He had no friends among the boys, who were all older and bigger than he was.

In 1811 Denmark was an ally of France in its war in Germany. Napoleon, the great French general, was Father's hero. In the hope of changing his luck, Mr. Andersen became a soldier.

The day his father left, Hans Christian was in bed with the measles. He would never forget the excitement of that day. Father sang and talked loudly.

Then he leaned over the bed and kissed Hans Christian hard.

"God bless you and care for you," he said in a husky voice.

Then the boy heard the drums beating and his mother weeping. She followed her husband to the city gate.

It was the first day of sorrow that Hans Christian had ever known. Grandma was there to sit beside him and hold his hand and wipe the tears from his eyes.

"He will be back," she said.

Father returned, unharmed, and went back to work at his bench, but he had a bad cough and was weak and tired — too tired even to read to the boy.

It was winter and the windows were frosted over. On one of them the frost looked like the form of a maiden with outstretched arms. In excitement Hans Christian pointed out the picture.

"It is the ice maiden," Father said. "Soon she will come to fetch me."

Hans Christian threw his arms about his father's knees. "No, no!" he cried, "I won't let her have you."

One evening the man woke in wild excitement, shouting of battles and of Napoleon.

"Napoleon has put me in command! I shall lead my men to victory!" he cried.

He tried to get out of bed. His face was red and his eyes were wild. His wife felt his cheek.

"He is burning with fever," she said to Hans Christian. "Go ask the wisewoman if he will get well."

Mother did not believe in doctors; instead she put her faith in wisewomen and fortune-tellers.

The wisewoman lived some distance from Odense. Hans Christian ran until he was breathless, then walked, then ran again.

He had seen the woman before. She had stopped at his home to talk with his mother. Hans Christian was afraid of her, for he thought that she looked like a witch.

Panting, he told her about his father. She measured Hans Christian's arm with a woolen thread and made strange signs with her hands. Then she pinned a green twig on his jacket.

"This," she said, "is a piece of the same kind of tree upon which the Saviour was crucified."

Hans Christian could not keep his teeth from chattering.

"Go now," she said. "Follow the river. If your father is to die, you will meet his ghost."

Hans Christian was so terrified he could

hardly make his shaking legs carry him. Yet he must make himself go home. He ran along the path which lay like a dim streak in the moonlight. He feared at every turn that he would see his father's ghost.

But he did not see it. When he arrived home his father was alive, but he still moaned and shouted, urging the men under his command to be brave in battle.

Three nights later he died.

Hans Christian lay beside his mother that night, but neither of them slept. All night long a cricket chirped. "Oh, hush!" Mother said. "He is dead. The ice maiden has fetched him."

Then Hans Christian remembered the picture the frost had formed on the window of a maiden with her arms outstretched.

Hans longed for his kind father with all of his heart. Now he was alone the whole day while Mother went out to do the washings. The longing was often a big ache inside him. He tried to amuse himself by playing with his puppet theater. But without his father there

at the bench to talk with him and to laugh at
the plays he made up, there was no fun in anything.

He had quickly learned to read during the
little time he had spent in school. Now he
took up *Arabian Nights* and the book of Holberg plays that his father had read to him so
often. He knew them by heart. With the aid
of his memory, he was able to follow the sense
of the printed words. In this way he taught
himself to read still better.

Although she did not have much time to
spend with her lonely son, his mother loved
him dearly. She taught him to keep himself
and his few clothes neat and clean.

Having no friends his own age, Hans Christian wandered about the neighborhood. He
talked with women who were working in their
gardens. One of these was Madame Bunkeflod, the widow of a minister. She invited him
into her house and gave him cookies and milk.

This was the first time the boy had been in
the home of an educated person. To him the
furniture and rooms seemed very fine. On

each side of the fireplace were shelves filled with books.

She saw him gazing at them. "Do you like books?" she asked.

"Oh, yes. My father had two books. I know them both by heart. I can read them, too."

"My brother was a poet," she said. "He is dead now. He is still famous."

She rose and put into Hans Christian's hands a book bound in red leather.

"My brother's best book of poems," she said.

Hans Christian was thrilled to know someone who was sister to a man who had written poetry.

"I make up plays," he said. "But I should like to write poems. Maybe some day I shall. I sit under the gooseberry bush in my mother's yard and make up tales."

"I have some work to do in the kitchen," she said. "Would you like to look at this book of Shakespeare's plays? It has pictures in it."

She handed him the book and left him alone in an easy chair. He found that he was able to read the plays and was at once in a new world. The exciting deeds, the ghosts and witches were just to his taste.

Madame Bunkeflod did not offer to let him take the book home with him. For days he went back to her house every afternoon.

"May I read the book?" he asked politely. She always smiled kindly when she let him in, and before he left, she always gave him cookies and milk. He thought her the nicest and the finest woman he had ever known.

Now he acted out Shakespeare's plays in his little puppet theater.

Soon he made up his first poem. It was about a servant girl who fell in love with a prince. He called it a poem, but there were no rhymes in it. Yet the lines were short, as they were in the book of poems Madame Bunkeflod had shown him. His spelling was terrible; so was his penmanship. But he was able to say that he had written a poem. And say it he did, to everyone he saw.

He took it to Madame Bunkeflod's house and read it to her.

"It is very good for a boy your age," she said.

To him this sounded like high praise. He went up and down the street reading his poem to all who would listen.

Next he wrote a poem about a king and queen. He was greatly pleased with himself.

CHAPTER 3

The New Boots

Not only was Hans Christian able to make up plays and write what he called poems, but he also had a high, beautiful voice. He liked to stand beside the house and sing songs his grandmother had taught him. People going by stopped to listen, and the neighbors next door came to stand by the fence.

So the days passed pleasantly enough, but he was often lonely in his strange little world. His mother worried that he was by himself so much.

28

"Our neighbor's son works in the cloth factory," she told him. "He brings home money each week and gives it to his mother. You are eleven years old. You should be at work to keep you out of mischief."

"I don't get into mischief."

"You might. Satan finds mischief for idle hands to do."

Mother asked Grandma to take him next morning to the factory.

"It's not only for the money," she said to Grandma. "If he is working, I'll know where he is and what he is doing."

When they reached the factory and Grandma saw the ragged, rough-looking boys he was to work with, she said, "It breaks my heart to see you among such people."

At first Hans Christian did not find his job as errand boy bad. Many of the workers were jolly men. They sang and joked and laughed.

"Can you sing?" someone asked the new boy.

"Oh, yes, I know many songs."

"Then sing for us," the man said.

29

Hans Christian sang again and again. The looms stood still and other boys were given the work he was supposed to do.

The men clapped their hands. Pleased with his audience, Hans Christian told them that he could act whole scenes from Shakespeare and Holberg.

A few days passed pleasantly enough. One

day he knew that he was singing very well. He was praised for his high, clear voice.

Then someone said, "It sounds like a girl's voice to me."

Everyone teased him until he ran from the building in tears.

"I will never go back there," he said.

"You need not go," Mother promised. "But you should do something with your time besides sewing for your puppets. You are so nimble with your fingers that you should become a tailor."

"I don't want to be a tailor. I shall become an actor."

"But see how well Mr. Dickman, the tailor, gets along. He has large windows, and men working for him, and a big house on the best street in town."

Hans Christian refused to take any interest in becoming a tailor. He went on playing with his puppet theater. His mother went on washing.

Two years after Hans Christian's father died, his mother remarried. The boy hated his stepfather on sight and scowled at the dark-haired man. A wave of longing for his own father swept over him. And he became jealous of the attention his mother paid to the stranger. The man was also a shoemaker and went to work at Father's workbench.

Soon Hans Christian's parents moved to a house by the river. Here his mother had a little garden in which the boy played. Nearby were great water wheels which he liked to watch as they turned. He could also watch his mother as she beat clothes with a stick near the rocky shore.

He liked to stand on one of the big rocks and sing at the top of his voice.

"You sing like an angel," said an old woman who washed clothes in the river. "Did you know that right under this spot lies China? It's possible that when you sing so loud and clear, the Chinese Prince can hear you."

This idea was enough to set his lively imagination to spinning fancies. Often on moonlight evenings he sat on the big rock, singing. As he sat he watched for the Chinese Prince to

dig himself up through the ground. He imag-
ined how this prince would carry him off to his
kingdom and make him rich and noble. Then
the prince would allow him to visit Odense
and build him a castle to live in there.

Hans Christian's habit of reading aloud his
poems and plays to all who would listen, of
singing, and of acting out plays he had learned
by heart earned him the attention of several
good families. He was invited into their
homes. Among those who took an interest in
him was Colonel Guldberg.

This man introduced him to Prince Christian, later to be King Christian the Eighth.
He lived in the castle at Odense.

Colonel Guldberg said, "If the prince
should ask you what you have a liking for, tell
him that you long to enter the grammar
school."

Hans Christian drew in his breath. He had
never dared to hope so high as the grammar
school. There only paying pupils were taken.

When he went before the prince, he was
asked what he could do. By way of reply, he

acted out a scene from Shakespeare. Then he sang.

The prince nodded his approval. "What do you plan to be when you become a man?"

"First I should like to go to the grammar school," Hans Christian said. "Then I shall become an actor or write plays or be a singer."

The prince put a hand to his mouth to hide a smile. "Study at grammar school is a long and costly course. You sing and recite well, but that is no mark of a genius. If you will take up something sensible like cabinetmaking, I will pay your expenses."

Hans Christian's heart fell. He did not want to become a cabinetmaker. Nor did he want to become a tailor as Mother wanted him to do.

Disappointed, he went home. Mother was heartsick that he would not be sent to the grammar school.

"Look at you," she said. "You are almost as tall as I am. You can't go on any longer without an object in life. You must go to the charity school."

At the charity school Hans Christian learned only religion, writing, and arithmetic. He could not spell or write a sentence clearly. He did no studying at home. Instead he learned his lessons on the way to and from school.

He made up strange stories in which he was always the hero. The boys thought him queer. No doubt they were jealous of him for they had heard that he went to fine homes to recite and sing.

One day a gang of them chased him, shouting, "There goes the playwriter!"

He hid in a corner at home and cried. This was the way shouting boys chased his weak-minded grandfather through the streets.

He told his mother that he would not go back to school. "Then," she said, "you must be confirmed. After that I will apprentice you to the tailor."

There were two classes for confirmation, the dean's and the chaplain's, at the church Hans Christian attended. Each child was allowed to choose which class he would attend. However, the richer children from the grammar school always went to the dean. The poor children from the charity school went to the chaplain. Yet Hans Christian chose to attend the dean's class.

"Why do you make trouble for yourself?" Mother asked. "The others will only look down upon you."

"I belong with them," the boy insisted. "The poor boys are rough and rude."

The children in the dean's class made him feel that he had pushed himself in where he did not belong. There was one girl, though, who always smiled at him, and one day she gave him a rose. He would never forget her nor that act of kindness.

An old seamstress made a confirmation coat for him. It was cut down from his dead father's suit. His stepfather made him a pair of boots. Hans Christian was very proud of them, for he had always worn wooden shoes.

He tucked his trousers down into the boot tops so that the boots would show better. Also, the boots squeaked. This pleased him for now everyone would be certain to notice them. When he marched up the aisle of the church his mind was upon his new boots. Then his conscience bothered him and he prayed for

forgiveness for not keeping his mind upon God. Then he thought again about his new boots.

Years later these boots would appear in his story, "The Red Shoes," in which Karen, who wears them, acts as he did then:

Everybody looked at her feet, and when she walked up the church to the chancel, she thought that even the old pictures, those portraits of dead and gone priests and their wives, with stiff collars and long black clothes, fixed their eyes upon her shoes. She thought of nothing else when the priest laid his hand upon her head and spoke to her of holy baptism, the covenant with God, and that from henceforth she was to be a responsible Christian person. The solemn notes of the organ resounded, the children sang with their sweet voices . . . but Karen only thought about her red shoes.

CHAPTER 4

Rough Going

Now that you are confirmed," said Mother, "you are ready to learn to be a tailor. You have such clever fingers that you will be a good one."

"But I don't want to be a tailor."

"Then what will you do? You are fourteen. It's time you were learning to do something to make a living."

"I am going to Copenhagen, the greatest city in the world."

"Copenhagen! What would you do there?"

"I will become famous. I know just how it is done. I have read about famous people. First they suffer a great deal. Then at last they become famous."

"Of course you'll not go off to Copenhagen! What a silly idea! How would you get there? How would you live?"

"I have money," Hans Christian said. "All my life I have been saving in the clay-pig bank that Grandma gave me for Christmas when I was little."

He broke open the clay pig and counted his money. In it were fourteen rix-dollars.*

Mother began to cry. Then Hans Christian, who wept very easily, broke into tears, too.

"You can't go. I will not allow it." She sobbed.

"But I must. Someday I will be famous."

Mother begged, but he would not change his mind.

Finally she sent him to get the wisewoman.

* A rix-dollar was a coin worth about a dollar.

The old woman came. She used coffee grounds and playing cards which she spread out on the table. She passed her hands over them and said strange words in a sing-song voice.

Then she pointed to Hans Christian and said in a shrill tone, "This boy will become a great man. In honor of him some day all of Odense will be lighted up."

At these words his mother broke into sobs, but Hans Christian laughed aloud.

At last Mother gave her permission for him to go to the big city. "But you will get no farther than Nyborg," she said. "When you see the Baltic Sea, you will become frightened. I know you will."

He knew that his good friend, the old printer Iversen, had become acquainted with actors and singers of the Royal Theater who had been in Odense a summer ago. Hans Christian had seen them perform. He went to Iversen.

"Will you please give me a letter of introduction to Madame Schall in Copenhagen?"

he asked politely. "I have heard she is a famous dancer."

The old printer looked surprised. "But I do not know Madame Schall," he said.

Hans Christian was disappointed.

"But you knew the actors who were here last summer. Surely some of them know Madame Schall. Please write me a letter to her. She will open the doors to fame for me. I know that she will."

The old printer wrote the letter. Hans Christian thanked him. On the way home he told everyone he saw that he was going to Copenhagen to become famous.

His mother packed his clothes in a small bundle and gave him a sack of lunch. She bargained with the driver of a post carriage to take him from the gates of Odense to the gates of Copenhagen for three rix-dollars. She walked with him to the gates of Odense. Grandma was standing there waiting. She threw her arms around his neck and sobbed, unable to speak.

Then the post carriage drove up and Hans

Christian climbed in. The man beside the
driver blew his horn. The driver cracked his
whip. The carriage started to roll. Hans
Christian waved to his weeping mother and
grandmother, then thrilled at every sight that
passed before his eyes.

He rode by coach for two days and nights.
When the driver stopped at small towns, the

43

other passengers went into the inns to eat. Hans Christian stood beside a wheel eating the dry bread his mother had given him. The smell of hot food made him hungry, but he must not spend any of his money.

When he arrived at Nyborg and saw the sea, a great longing for home swept over him. He boarded the ferry feeling lost and alone. Now he had no one but God to lean upon.

As soon as he landed at Zealand, he stepped behind a shed on shore and sank to his knees and prayed to God to guide him and protect him.

That whole day and the next night he rode in the post carriage through cities and villages. A kindly lady, seeing how lonely he looked, spoke to him and gave him part of her lunch.

On Monday morning, September 5, 1819, he saw from a hilltop the great city of Copenhagen spread before his eyes. Prickles of excitement ran up and down his spine.

He left the carriage at the gates of the city, for his fare was paid only that far. With his little bundle in his hand he entered the city.

He walked until he came to a small inn where he engaged a room. He had only ten rix-dollars in his pocket. He would quickly have to find a way to earn some money. Yet he decided not to worry about that until tomorrow. He found his way to the Royal Theater and walked around it several times. He touched the walls fondly, almost imagining this place as his home.

The next day he dressed himself in his confirmation suit. He put on the squeaky boots and a hat so large it came down over his ears. He carefully put his letter of introduction to Madame Schall in a pocket.

Before he rang her bell, he fell on his knees and prayed that here he might find help. When he rose to his feet, a maidservant came down the steps with a basket on her arm. She smiled at him and handed him a coin.

Hans Christian thought he looked very fine in his confirmation clothes. How then could the maid mistake him for a beggar?

He called after her to take her money.

"Keep it, keep it, boy," she called back. Then she was gone.

A servant led him before Madame Schall. She was small and beautiful, with the pinkest cheeks he had ever seen. He handed her the printer's letter.

"But I've never heard of this man!" she exclaimed.

"Oh, he's a very good man. He's a printer in Odense. He knows many of the actors of the Royal Theater who were in our city last summer."

"Well," she said, "what is it you want?"

"I want your help, great lady. I want to become an actor."

"What can you do?"

"I can do *Cinderella*," he replied. "I saw the ballet last summer. I know it by heart."

"Let me see you do a scene or two," the dancer said.

Hans Christian pulled off his boots. "So I can dance better," he explained.

Using his broad hat as a tambourine he danced around the room, singing. The lady looked startled at his awkward, strange antics as he acted the part of Cinderella.

"I'm sorry. I can do nothing for you," she said.

His heart fell and he turned his back to her as he pulled on his boots. He did not want her to see the tears in his eyes.

He next went to see the manager of the theater. "I can sing, dance, and act," Hans Christian said.

"You are too thin for the stage," the man told him.

Hans replied, "If you hire me for one hundred rix-dollars a month, then I shall soon get fat."

The man stared at him and then said, "We hire only people of education."

It was as though the man had run a sword through Hans Christian's heart. He turned away and left the theater to roam the streets. In all this big city, there was no one to help him.

Then he remembered what he had read about great people. "This is the way it always is," he spoke aloud. "First one must suffer greatly, then at last he becomes famous."

Feeling better, he bought a gallery ticket for the opera of *Paul and Virginia*. When the lovers in the story became separated, Hans Christian was so touched that he burst into tears.

"Don't cry," said the woman beside him. "It is only a play." She gave him a sandwich to comfort him.

Then he told her and others who were listening that he had come to Copenhagen to become an actor but no one would help him. One of the women gave him another sandwich and an apple to cheer him up.

CHAPTER 5

Discouragement

The next morning, after he paid for his room, Hans Christian counted his money and found that he had but one rix-dollar left. He had never felt so lonely or hopeless in his life. He must either get a job or find some ship on which he could work his way back to Odense. He shuddered at the thought of going back to his home town.

There people would laugh at him for having set out with such grand ideas of becoming famous.

He bought a newspaper and found that a cabinetmaker needed an apprentice. He remembered that when he had asked Prince Christian to send him to the grammar school, the prince had advised him to become a cabinetmaker.

In order to become apprenticed he must send for his record of baptism and a recommendation. The kindly carpenter told Hans Christian that he could stay at his house while he was waiting for these.

Early the next morning Hans Christian went to the workshop. He was so tall, thin, awkward, and homely that the workmen laughed rudely as soon as they saw him. His face turned red and tears came to his eyes. Finding he was so easily hurt, the workers turned on him the full force of their teasing. By noon the boy had had enough. He told the cabinetmaker that he could not stay.

Taking his little bundle of clothes he set

out to roam the streets, wondering what was to become of him. He bought a bun and munched it as he walked. He went to the harbor at the foot of the street and stared at the ships. He thought again of finding one that would take him back to Odense. At last, though, he knew that he could not go back to the laughter of the townspeople. He would rather starve.

Suddenly he straightened up. A memory had awakened in him. He remembered having read in an Odense newspaper the name of a gentleman named Siboni. The man was the head of the music academy in Copenhagen.

People had praised Hans Christian's voice. Perhaps Mr. Siboni would help him. He asked the way to the singer's home and went there.

It happened that Mr. Siboni was having a dinner party. The composer Weyse was there and the poet Baggesen. The housekeeper opened the door. At once Hans Christian poured out his story. In fact, he told her nearly the whole story of his life, and all about his ambitions.

She listened to him kindly, then told him to wait. She was gone so long that Hans Christian thought she must have repeated all he had told her. When she returned, Mr. Siboni and all of his guests were with her.

"I hear you want to be a singer," said Mr. Siboni. "Sing for us."

Hans Christian sang, then recited some scenes from Holberg.

The poet Baggesen said, "I believe that something will some day come out of him." Then he turned to the boy. "Do not be vain when some day the whole public applauds you."

Mr. Siboni said, "You have a very pure and beautiful voice. Sleep here tonight. The housekeeper will show you to your bed. Tomorrow you may go to Professor Weyse, who will help you."

Professor Weyse had been a poor boy himself and his heart had been touched by Hans Christian's story and his shabby appearance.

He had taken up a fine collection among Siboni's dinner guests and had seventy rix-dollars for the boy. He told him that the great Siboni would train him as a singer. He advised him to go out and find a room for which he must not pay over sixteen rix-dollars a month. He could eat with Mr. Siboni's kitchen help.

When the boy went out into the street, he wanted to jump and shout with joy. Yet, this was the way he had known it would be. To him it was entirely natural that doors would open this easily for him.

Mr. Siboni was an emotional man, and often his pupil's singing made him wildly unhappy. His cheeks turned red and his eyes flashed and he burst out scolding in German, his native tongue.

At such times Hans Christian became so frightened that he trembled. Often Mr. Siboni's stern look made the boy's voice shake and tears come to his eyes.

"Come now," Mr. Siboni would say. "Do not be frightened. I shall not beat you."

The boy wrote to his mother, bragging that the great Siboni had taken him as a pupil and that the poet Baggesen had said that he, Hans Christian, would some day be applauded by the whole public. He well knew that his mother would read this letter to all of the neighbors.

He did not tell his mother that he lived in a miserable house in a poor neighborhood, that his room was nothing more than a closet, without a window, and that the only air came from holes in the door. The room was so small that he had to put the one straight chair on the bed in order to move around.

He suffered during the bitter winter. His shoes were worn out and he used folded newspapers inside the soles. He had no warm underwear and his jacket was thin. He came down with a bad cold and coughed for the rest of the winter.

Mr. Siboni taught him for six months, then said, "I am sorry, but you will never become a fine singer. Go back to your home and learn a trade."

Those hateful words again! Learn a trade.
He would starve first!

Crushed in spirit, he returned to his little
box of a room. His shoulders drooped as he
sat on the edge of the bed. Now which way
could he turn? The room grew dark. Sigh-
ing, he rose to light his candle. As the match
flared, the flame seemed to warm his heart
for an instant. And at the moment was sown
in his mind the scene which would some day

appear in one of his best-loved tales, "The Little Match Girl":

Her little hands were almost dead with cold. Oh, one little match would do some good! Dared she pull one out of the bundle and strike it on the wall to warm her fingers? She pulled one out, "ritsch." How it spluttered, how it blazed! It burnt with a bright clear flame, just like a little candle when she held her hand round it. It was a very curious candle too. The little girl fancied that she was sitting in front of a big stove with polished brass feet and handles. There was a splendid fire blazing in it and warming her so beautifully, but . . . just as she was stretching out her feet to warm them, the blaze went out, the stove vanished, and she was left sitting with the end of the burnt-out match in her hand.

So it was with Hans Christian. Like the little match girl, his imagination would kindle one warm dream after another to keep him from despair.

As he sat there on his bed staring at the

candle and with the burnt end of the match still in his hand, suddenly a name popped into his mind — Guldberg. In Odense Colonel Guldberg had shown him much kindness and had introduced him to the prince.

Hans Christian now remembered that Colonel Guldberg had said that he had a brother who was a poet and professor who lived in Copenhagen.

The boy borrowed paper from his landlady and wrote Professor Guldberg a letter. He told the man of his struggles and of his ambitions.

While he waited for an answer, he amused himself with his toy theater he had built from an old box. Instead of paying good money to have his shoes soled he had bought little dolls. These he dressed with scraps of bright cloth which he had begged from a seamstress.

No answer came to his letter, so Hans Christian went to see Professor Guldberg. There was a kindly twinkle in the man's blue eyes when the boy entered his study, warm with the books which lined the walls.

"So you are the one who came to Copenhagen to seek your fortune?" the man asked with a chuckle. "It would seem that you did not spend much time in school. You cannot spell nor write a clear sentence."

"But," Hans Christian put in, "I want to be an actor. I do not need much learning. I can read well and learn parts quickly."

He then recited a scene from Holberg.

"You do have some ability," Professor Guldberg said. "I shall see if Lindgron, the best comic actor at the theater, will teach you how to act."

At Professor Guldberg's request Lindgron took Hans Christian as a pupil. The boy begged to be given a tragedy to learn. He recited this so well that the old man slapped him on the shoulder and said, "Feeling you do have; but you must not be an actor, though God knows what else."

"Why must I not be an actor?"

"You have no grace. You have no looks. God did not create you to be an actor."

Hans Christian was afraid that the old man

would tell him to be sensible and go out and learn a trade. The boy hurried away before he would have to listen to the hated words again.

He went back to Professor Guldberg in tears.

"Do not worry," the professor said. "There are other things you can do, I am sure."

CHAPTER 6

The End
of the World

At Professor Guldberg's home Hans Christian first met the dancer Dahlen. This man's wife was the finest ballet dancer on the Danish stage. The two of them were very kind to the stage-struck boy.

Dahlen took him to his dancing school which was run in connection with the theater. Hans Christian stood by the exercise bar and stretched his legs by the hour. Soon

Dahlen told him that he would never become a dancer.

"I will work very hard," Hans Christian promised.

Dahlen shook his head. "Hard work is not enough. You do not have the form nor the grace."

Hans Christian swallowed the lump in his throat. He was this close to the theater. It seemed to him that he had just got his toe inside its magic doorway. He continued to exercise every day with the dancing students.

One night an operetta was being given. Hans Christian heard that during this performance everyone who had anything to do with the dancing school would be needed on the stage during the market scene.

He put his great coat he had worn for his confirmation back on. He always took it off while he exercised. It barely held together by this time, but it was always carefully brushed and neatly mended.

Along with the rest of the extras he painted his cheeks and was happily excited. Yet when he followed the crowd upon the stage, the joy of at last being in front of the footlights was dimmed by the knowledge that his waistcoat and sleeves and trousers were too short. He did not dare stand up straight for fear people would notice how short his waistcoat was. Then all at once the thrill of being on the stage swept over him. His heart beat fast and he forgot his shabby clothes and stepped forward.

One of the leading singers saw him.

"I wish you happiness on your debut," the singer said jeeringly.

He took Hans Christian's hand and led him forward to the footlights. "Allow me to introduce you to the Danish public," he said. The audience broke into a roar of laughter at Hans Christian's ridiculous appearance.

He jerked his hand away and fled from the stage with tears streaming down his cheeks. Never had he been so unhappy.

"Dry your eyes, son," Dahlen told him kindly. "The world has not come to an end."

"But they laughed at me!" he wailed.

"Everyone worth his salt has been laughed at sometime in his life," Dahlen said. "I'm soon putting on a ballet I wrote myself. I'll give you a small part in it."

Instantly Hans Christian was happy again.

He was given the part of a troll among other trolls, and he was able to shed his shabby clothes and dress in green tights. He knew that his costume displayed his long arms and legs, but he managed to stay in the middle of the group so that the audience would not make fun of him.

His name was printed on the program. He treasured this piece of paper and looked at it time and again. He took it to bed with him at night and stared at his name by candle-light.

One day he suddenly remembered the girl who had given him the rose when all the other students were snubbing him in confirmation class. She had gone to live in Copenhagen. He told the Dahlens about her, and was surprised to find that they knew Miss Tonder-Lund. They urged him to visit her.

He felt out of place going to such a fine house in his shabby clothes, but he rang the bell and was let in. He was surprised to find Miss Tonder-Lund a young lady, but she knew him at once and shook his hand warmly.

"You are the boy in my confirmation class," she said. "Hans Christian Andersen!"

"And you are the kind girl who gave me a rose. I have never forgotten you."

They quickly became good friends and she and her sister took him into their circle of people of high rank. They found him amusing when he read to them the poems and plays he had written.

Some of them gave him little gifts of money. One man gave him a blue coat of good material, with shiny buttons. Hans Christian thought he looked very grand in this garment. There was one thing wrong. It was much too big across the chest. To remedy this matter Hans Christian stuffed the front with folded theater programs.

He had a notion that what he did on New Year's Day would be what he would do during the year. His greatest wish was to have a part in a play.

No one had invited him to be a guest on that holiday and he was very lonely. He went to the theater. It was closed and the entrance was being guarded by a half-blind watchman. The boy tiptoed past him, up the dusty stairs, and onto the stage.

He held out his arms and tried to think of a part to act. His mind was blank. He sank to his knees and said the Lord's Prayer aloud. He arose, feeling sure that within the year he would be given a part in a play.

During the two years he had lived in Copenhagen, he had never been out into the open country. In early spring of the third

year he went to the garden of the summer home of King Frederick the Sixth. The castle was within walking distance of the city and the garden was open to the public when the king was not there.

It was a sunny spring day. The grass was green. Flowers bloomed. Suddenly he stood still under a budding beech tree. The world was so beautiful that happiness flooded his heart. He shouted aloud for joy and threw his arms about the tree and kissed it.

"Is he crazy?" he heard a voice behind him ask. It was one of the gardeners of the castle.

He ran away thinking of his grandfather. Was he, Hans Christian, perhaps also weak in the head to have done such a thing?

One day the leader of the theater's chorus school heard him singing and asked him to become a member of the chorus.

Hans Christian quickly grasped at this straw. Perhaps it might be a steppingstone to the stage. The singing school became his whole life and his lessons suffered. Professor Guldberg was teaching him Danish grammar and he had hired a tutor to teach him Latin. This study the boy found very boring. Some of his fellow students in the singing school told him that Latin was not needed for chorus work. As a result he often skipped his evening Latin lesson.

Now he was given parts in operettas and wore costumes. It did not bother him too much that often these costumes were tights. His long, skinny arms and legs looked even more ridiculous than when he wore looser clothes. In one performance he wore flesh-colored tights and a blond wig with a braid down his back. Someone told him that he looked like a skinned cat, but he was able to laugh at this remark. He was part of the theater and that was what mattered. As a student he was allowed to sit in one of the cheapest seats to watch other plays.

Professor Guldberg heard that he was skipping his Latin classes and sent for him.

The man looked stern as he puffed on his pipe. He glared at the boy from under dark, bushy eyebrows.

"I—I'm sorry," Hans Christian stammered.

"I'm through with you!" Guldberg roared. "I placed so much hope in you. But you are a rattlebrain. You won't do what is best for you."

"I will work harder. I promise . . ."

"I'm done with you. I still have thirty rix-dollars from the fund Professor Weyse collected for you. You may come and get ten rix-dollars of that each month until it is gone. You are not worth helping further."

Hans Christian felt so crushed that he wanted to drop to the floor.

"Oh, please!" he begged, the tears streaming down his cheeks.

"There, you are acting again," Professor Guldberg said. "Do not act any more comedy. Go now!"

Hans Christian stumbled from the room feeling that the end of the world had come for him.

CHAPTER 7

Visit to Odense

Hans Christian now had a room at the home of a widow named Madame Jurgensen. She gave him breakfast. Before noon he would leave the house and his land-lady thought he was going to the home of one of his friends for dinner.

Instead he went to sit on a bench in the park. Sometimes he had saved a piece of bread to munch. Most of the time he went hungry. From time to time he got up to stamp his cold feet.

His work in the chorus was poorly paid. In three months the thirty rix-dollars Professor Guldberg had given him of the money Professor Weyse had collected was gone. The winter he was seventeen was one of bitter hardship for Hans Christian. He suffered from cold, hunger, and hopelessness. His shoes were cracked and had holes in the soles. He developed a racking cough which spoiled his singing voice.

At last spring came and with it new hope. Hans Christian decided to write a tragedy in verse. When he was finished, he took it to read to Madame Rahbek, a kind lady he had met at Miss Tonder-Lund's. When he was leaving to call upon another friend to read his masterpiece to her, Madame Rahbek handed him a bouquet of roses.

"Take these to Madame von Colbjornsen, please," she said. "She will enjoy receiving them from the hands of a poet."

No doubt Madame Rahbek spoke in a

joking manner, but the words sent a thrill to the core of Hans Christian's being. At that moment was born in him the ambition to become a writer and a poet. Up to this time writing his little poems and plays had been merely an amusement. Now he would set to work in earnest and win fame with his pen.

He decided to write another tragedy. He would offer it to the Royal Theater, and with the money he earned he would study.

*Within two weeks he finished "Robbers in Wissenberg." He took the play to Miss Tonder-Lund.

After reading it she said, "There is scarcely a correctly spelled word in this manuscript. I'll correct it for you and have it written so those directors of the Royal Theater will be able to read it."

In six weeks the tragedy was sent back with a letter from the theater directors which he read and reread, looking for some little ray of hope. The letter said that his piece was completely unsuitable for the stage — that his lack of education showed on every page. The directors advised him to seek help from his friends in getting the learning without which the career he was so eager to adopt must ever be closed to him.

It was the end of the theatrical season, in May, 1822. Usually at this season of the year Hans Christian was bubbling with the joy of living, but he was soon to receive another blow. A letter came from the theater directors telling him that he was being dismissed from the singing and dancing schools.

Now he felt once again cast into a wide, heartless world. There was no one to help him — no one to support him. But he did not waste time feeling sorry for himself. He knew that he must write a play for the Royal Theater, and it *must* be accepted.

He chose a subject based on a happening in history and called the play he wrote "Alfsol." He was so pleased with the first act that he felt that he must show it to someone. He had heard of Captain Wulff who was noted for his Danish translation of Shakespeare.

Hans Christian hurried to the captain's home. When he was taken to the room where the man sat eating his breakfast, Hans Christian said quickly, "You have translated Shakespeare. I admire him greatly. I, too, am a playwright. I have written a tragedy. I shall read it to you."

The captain stifled a smile. "First have breakfast with me," he invited.

"No, thank you," Hans Christian replied. "I'll read to you while you eat."

When he had finished, Hans Christian asked breathlessly, "Do you think I shall amount to anything? I wish it so much."

"It's a little soon to tell," Captain Wulff said. He rose as if to show that the visit was ended. "Come again," he said politely.

"Yes, I will, when I have a new tragedy written."

"That will be a long time, then," the man said.

"In about two weeks I will have another one written," Hans Christian said as the captain closed the door.

Soon Hans Christian was invited to dine with Captain Wulff and his family. He became good friends with them and often visited at their home.

One of Hans Christian's friends was a preacher named Gutfeldt. Of course the young writer showed him his "Alfsol." Mr. Gutfeldt corrected it and sent it, along with a letter of recommendation, to the Royal Theater.

During the summer Hans Christian hung between hope and fear. He suffered bitter want and was always hungry, but he was too proud to tell his friends of his plight. Yet he was not unhappy, for a new world had opened to him. He had discovered the books of Sir Walter Scott. Often he gave to the lending library the money he should have spent for food.

When weeks passed without his hearing about his play, Mr. Gutfeldt told him that he should go to the home of State Counsellor Jonas Collin, the main director of the Royal Theater. He was one of the finest and most famous men in Denmark and had been known to help talented and deserving young people.

Hans Christian found Jonas Collin to be a noble-looking man with an air of dignity. He let the boy do most of the talking and watched him gravely as he chattered on. Hans Christian left, feeling that the great man had little sympathy for him.

Yet in a few days Hans Christian was sent for by the directors of the theater. Mr. Rahbek, another of the theater directors, handed him back his play. "It is useless for the theater," he said, "but now and then we saw glints of gold in it. We hope that by hard study you may some day be able to write a work worthy of being acted on the Danish stage."

There it was again! People were always telling him he must study. Now he was ready to believe it. But how was he to study without money, without even enough food?

Soon he received the answer to his questions. Counsellor Collin sent for him. The boy entered the man's study with his heart beating fast.

The counsellor came to the point at once. "I have recommended you to King Frederick. He gives financial aid to gifted persons. He is granting you a certain sum each year for as long as I advise that you get it. You will receive free instruction at the grammar school at Slagelse, twelve miles from here. You will go there by the earliest mail carriage."

For once Hans Christian was dumb with surprise.

Mr. Collin went on, "I shall send you the money for your needs. Write to me at any time. Tell me how things go with you."

Hans Christian grasped Mr. Collin's hand and squeezed it in thanks. Tears streamed down his face.

From that time on Counsellor Collin was like a father to Hans Christian.

It was a golden autumn day when he set out in the mail coach for Slagelse. He thrilled with the excitement of beginning a new adventure. He wished that Father and

Grandma were still alive so that they could hear of his good fortune. As soon as he arrived at Slagelse, he went to the little inn and wrote a long letter to his mother. He told her that now that the gateway to an education had opened for him, he was on his way to greatness.

The first afternoon he was in the town, he asked the innkeeper what there was to see there.

"A new English fire engine and Pastor Bastholm's library and the little theater," the innkeeper answered proudly.

It was, Hans Christian found, a sleepy village where there was nothing to do for amusement except attend the rehearsals of the theater.

He found room and board with a middle-aged widow. He had a pleasant little room that overlooked a garden and a field.

In grammar school at seventeen he was like a wild bird in a cage. He had a great wish to learn, but during the first few days he floundered about, feeling like one thrown

into the sea. One wave followed another: geography, grammar, arithmetic, history. He felt that he would never be able to learn all of them.

He knew nothing and was put into the beginners' class. He loomed far above his fellow students in height and had to jackknife onto the bench behind the desk. He knew that everyone was laughing at him.

He quickly earned the dislike of Rector Meisling, his teacher. The rector had a good mind, but he was ugly, untidy, and disagreeable. Foolishly Hans Christian went to call upon him. He told the rector and his wife of his hopes and ambitions and read them some of his writings.

"Trash!" Rector Meisling exploded. "Nothing but trash!"

Hans Christian cringed.

However, by hard work, Hans Christian earned some good grades. While on a visit with the Collin family in Copenhagen, he went to call upon Professor Guldberg, once his teacher and guardian, and showed him his report card. Guldberg praised him, and the boy felt that they were friends again.

"I beg you, though," the professor added, "not to write any more verses. Put all of your energy into your studies."

This was advice that the boy was to receive on all sides. Grateful that he once again had the professor's friendship, Hans Christian thanked him for his advice.

Soon afterward, Hans Christian received a letter from Colonel Guldberg, Professor Guldberg's brother. Hans Christian well remembered how the colonel had encouraged him in Odense. His old friend was very pleased that the boy had been admitted to the grammar school, and he invited Hans Christian to visit him at Odense. He offered to pay the traveling expenses.

Hans Christian, however, would not take advantage of the kind offer. He accepted only enough money to take the ferry across the Baltic Sea, and then he walked the rest of the way. His heart was filled with happiness. When he came close enough to the town to see the church tower, he burst into tears.

He had a touching meeting with his old mother. She was still doing washings in the stream that went by the house. The cold water gave her rheumatism, and as a remedy for the pain she often sipped from the brandy bottle she carried in her pocket.

Hans Christian greatly missed his grandmother, who had died the year after he left

Odense. His harmless, insane grandfather was also dead.

As he walked up the streets, he saw that people opened their windows to look at him. He was proud that he had fared well enough to have attracted attention. How glad he was now that he had not taken a boat back to Odense when he was penniless! How people would have laughed at him then!

One afternoon he was taken with the families of the Guldbergs and the Bishop of Odense to go sailing on the stream.

When he returned, his mother cried for joy. "You were honored like the child of a count," she said.

CHAPTER 8

The Ugly Duckling

When Hans Christian returned to Slagelse, the uplift of spirits he had felt at his brief moment of glory vanished. He worked very hard. Soon he was put into a higher class, but here he felt greater pressure being put upon him. He studied late into the night. When he became sleepy, he dashed cold water on his head or ran around the garden until he was awake enough to understand what he was trying to learn.

Yet, no matter how hard he tried, Rector

Meisling made him the mark of his crude jokes and insults. Whenever Hans Christian entered the rector's room, he became stiff with fear. His anxiety often caused him to say just the opposite of what he intended. This aroused the cruel rector to still greater depths of abuse.

Hans Christian became so discouraged that he wrote to the headmaster. He said, "I regard myself a person so little gifted by nature that it is impossible for me to study. The people of Copenhagen have thrown away the money they spent upon me."

The headmaster sent for him and talked to him kindly. "You are making good progress," he said. "Continue to work hard. I know what you are going through. I myself was a peasant youth of three-and-twenty when I commenced my studies."

Every Sunday the pupils had to attend Sunday school. Most of them took their schoolbooks along and learned their lessons in history and mathematics during the sermon. Hans Christian studied his lesson in religion, thinking it less sinful to study that subject in such a setting.

Although Rector Meisling seemed to have taken a dislike to Hans Christian, the boy was always invited to his house on Sunday afternoons. There the man was a different person. He told jokes and laughed, set up tin soldiers, and played with the pupils and his children.

Other than the gay Sunday afternoons at the Meisling home, Hans Christian's only amusement was the rehearsals in the little theater nearby. Here he could again lose himself for a time in the world of stage make-believe.

Always he had the gift for making friends among important and wellborn people. Among the good friends he had met in Odense was Ingemann the poet. He had just married and was teaching in an academy for the nobility near Slagelse.

When Mr. Ingemann and his bride invited Hans Christian to their home, he was overjoyed. There it seemed to him life was like a beautiful story. There were shelves of books in beautiful bindings. On the walls were pictures of poets. Flowers and vines twined around the windows, and the lawn sloped down to a lake.

The Ingemanns took him to sail on the lake. An aeolian harp was fastened to the mast, and the breeze played pleasant music upon it.

This was a friendship that would endure through the years. Every summer Hans Christian would be a welcome guest at their home. He really loved these friends. Later he wrote of them, "There are people in whose society one is made better . . . that which is bitter passes away, and the whole world appears in sunlight."

Hans Christian had need of friends such as the Ingemanns. Rector Meisling continued to abuse him. The boy usually knew his lessons perfectly, but when the rector called upon him to recite, the smaller boys could feel the bench shake, and the answers never came out as Hans Christian wished them to. Then Rector Meisling would roar, "You are a hopeless fool! You will never amount to anything!"

Hans Christian himself had never been jealous of anyone. He had no idea that the rector was jealous of him because he was welcome in the homes of people of importance. The shabby schoolmaster and his wife yearned to be accepted by such people.

Yet the boy got good grades. Usually his mark on conduct was "Remarkably good." One term his conduct was marked "Very good." He was crushed by this drop.

At Christmas he made another visit to Copenhagen. He dreaded showing this report card to Mr. Collin. "The counsellor will think I am wasting the people's money," he thought.

To his surprise Mr. Collin said, "Good! This shows that you have been working hard. I know it took courage for a big boy like you to be in classes with pupils so much younger."

The Collin household was beginning to seem like home; the friendly family seemed like his own. Ingeborg, the oldest daughter, treated him like a brother. The oldest son, Edvard, who had become his idol, gave him a book. The three smaller children treated him like one of themselves. Mr. Collin loaned him money for a new coat.

This Christmas visit to Copenhagen was entirely happy.

Hans Christian had received a small

amount of money from his grandmother's estate. It amounted to only twenty rix-dollars, but for a brief time he felt quite rich to have money of his own.

He repaid Mr. Collin for the coat and sent some money to his mother. The counsellor was well pleased that his ward had shown this sense of responsibility.

With what was left, Hans Christian bought himself some new underwear, and three books. These, with the one Edvard had given him, were the only books he had ever owned, and to him they seemed like treasures.

Hans Christian dreaded returning to school. It had been like being let out of prison to be away from Rector Meisling's cruel scoldings. No matter how hard he tried, Hans Christian did not fit into Meisling's pattern of the ideal pupil. He poured out his unhappiness and despair each evening in his diary.

Later these experiences would become his masterpiece, "The Ugly Duckling," in which he wrote:

But the poor duckling which had been the last to come out of the shell, and who was so ugly, was bitten, pushed about, and made fun of both by the ducks and the hens. "He is too big," they all said; and the turkey-cock, who was born with his spurs on, and therefore thought himself quite an emperor, puffed himself up like a vessel in full sail, made for him, and gobbled and gobbled till he became quite red in the face. The poor duckling was at his wit's end, and did not know which way to turn; he was in despair because he was so ugly, and the butt of the whole duckyard.

. . . .

"I think I will go out into the wide world," said the duckling.*

Much as Hans Christian longed to take wing and fly into the wide world, he could not do so. He must remain in this world where no one understood him or his strange longings to do something which would bring him fame.

* See pages 178–191 for the complete story.

CHAPTER 9

Escape

 Hans Christian was nearly twenty when his luck turned for the worse. Meisling took a post as rector in the grammar school in nearby Helsingor. He wrote to Counsellor Collin saying that he was willing to take Hans Christian with him and would give him lessons in Latin and Greek. This would enable the young man to take the entrance examinations for Copenhagen

University in half a year, which would not be the case if he stayed behind in Slagelse.

The rector did not mention the advantages to himself of having the boy in his home. He would get the two hundred rix-dollars allowed for board and room. Also, he would have a kindly person to help take care of his unruly children.

Hans Christian had been unhappy before. Now in the Meisling home he was miserable. He had been poor all of his life, but his mother had always kept their little home neat and clean. He himself was a tidy person. Now he lived amid dirt and clutter and with people who quarreled most of the time.

He managed to keep his own room in order, and this place was his only refuge. Now he must bear Rector Meisling's scoldings not only during school but also while he was at home.

To add to his unhappiness he learned that his mother had been put in the poorhouse. How he longed to be able to do something for her!

While he lived with Rector Meisling, Hans Christian did not go to visit anyone. The Meislings had no friends, and their boarder had no way of getting acquainted with anyone.

His life with this family would be like a bad dream in his memory. He lost all confidence in himself. Because of the rector's constant scoldings, he felt himself the most ugly, the most stupid person on earth.

His letters to Counsellor Collin showed his unhappiness.

Mr. Collin wrote:

> Don't lose courage, my dear Andersen! Compose your mind and be quiet and reasonable; you will see that all will go well; the Rector bears good will to you. He takes perhaps another way of showing it from what others would, but still it leads to the same end. . . . God bless you!
>
> Yours,
Collin

The only highlight of his life then was his yearly Christmas vacation in Copenhagen.

What a treat it was to get out of the rector's house and into the Wulffs' home where he had been invited to spend the holidays! Here was cleanliness and luxury. The Wulff family lived in part of a castle. The big room where Hans Christian stayed overlooked the square. He looked down upon it and said aloud, "Here I came as a poor lad." His soul filled with thankfulness for his change in fortune.

Mrs. Wulff was as kind as a mother to him, and the Wulff children treated him like one of the family. Mrs. Wulff tried to correct his awkward manners and told him that he must not always blurt out the first thing that came into his head.

In this home Hans Christian met a number of famous men. Among them was the poet Adam Oehlenschlager. Hans Christian heard praise of the poet from the lips of everyone. Then came an evening that would linger in his memory forever. In a brilliantly lighted drawing room Oehlenschlager read his poems aloud.

Aware of the shabbiness of his clothes in contrast with the beautifully dressed guests, Hans Christian hid behind the long curtains. Oehlenschlager saw him, drew the curtains aside, and shook hands with him, saying, "I hear that you write poetry, too. I should like to hear something you have written."

Hans Christian wanted to fall on his knees

before the great man. "I have written a poem, 'The Dying Child,'" he confessed. "I'll read it to you, if you wish."

And read it he did.

"It shows feeling," Oehlenschlager said kindly. Hans Christian felt as though he were floating on air.

The happy days flew all too quickly, and

then he was back in the rector's home, which in contrast to the Wulffs' seemed like a pig-pen.

The rector had also just come from Copenhagen, but had not been invited to any homes of gifted people.

His eyes were slits of jealous anger as he stared at his pupil. "I heard that you made a fool of yourself," he growled, "that you read aloud to Oehlenschlager a poem you had written. You must be crazy!"

"He asked me to read it," Hans Christian defended himself.

Rector Meisling glared at his pupil. "Bring me the poem," he commanded. "If I find in it one spark of poetry, I shall forgive you."

Hans Christian's hands were shaking as he handed the piece of paper to the rector.

Meisling's face turned red, and his voice trembled as he roared, "Utter trash! It's not worth the paper it's written upon! Have I been wasting my time and talent trying to teach a stupid animal who throws away his time on such nonsense?"

From that day on Hans Christian's situation became worse. The rector heaped abuse and ridicule upon him until the young man felt that he could not stand this state of affairs any longer. He later wrote, "That was the darkest, the most unhappy time in my life."

Rector Meisling even begrudged him the food he ate and served him only the smallest portions. Now hunger was added to his other sufferings. Once again he was as starved as he had been in the old days in Copenhagen.

However, at this time a young teacher came to visit the school. He saw the small helpings of food and heard the rector shout that Hans Christian was a stupid fool who would never amount to anything. He saw how Hans Christian cringed and shook with terror every time the rector yelled at him.

The young teacher made it a point to call upon Counsellor Collin when he was in Copenhagen and told him of Rector Meisling's mistreatment of his ward.

4465
VALLEY PARK
ELEMENTARY LIBRARY

Mr. Collin wrote to Hans Christian, telling him to leave the rector's house at once.

After he had packed his few clothes, Hans Christian went to say good-by. He held out his hand, but Rector Meisling ignored it. "You miserable boy!" he shouted. "You will never become a student. You fancy yourself a poet. Your poems will grow moldy on the floor of a bookseller's store. You will end your days in a madhouse!"

The angry rector stamped out of the room, leaving Hans Christian feeling as though a terrible curse had been laid upon him. Was he indeed to become a lunatic like his old grandfather?

Trembling to his innermost being, Hans Christian left the miserable house where he had been so unhappy and took the stage for Copenhagen.

As soon as he saw the gateway to the city, his spirits picked up. Surely he could never again be as unhappy as he had been during the time he was with Rector Meisling. Now his luck must turn for the better.

He stayed with the Collins for a few days. Here he would always feel truly at home.

Then a little garret room was rented for him. It had a bed, a table, a chair, a shelf for his books, a tiny stove, and a round, braided rug. Here, he said, the moon often visited him. Now there was no one to scold or find fault with him. His spirit soared like a bird set free.

Counsellor Collin found a tutor for him,

a young man named Muller who would later win fame for his knowledge of northern languages and of history.

The counsellor gave Hans Christian a set sum for his support. Since he was expected to pay his tutor out of this amount, he had to save money in other ways.

It was the custom then in Copenhagen for wealthy families to invite poor students to have dinner with them. Hans Christian had the gift for making friends and soon had regular eating places for every day in the week. He liked being able to see how different families lived. These opportunities would have an influence on his own personality, he who had had so little chance to learn the gracious ways of living.

CHAPTER 10

First Success

Hans Christian was blissfully happy to be back in Copenhagen again. Freed from Rector Meisling's power and from the school bench, Hans Christian's mind began soaking up knowledge. Now he could express himself like a free person.

He spoke of Mr. Muller as the noblest and most kindly of human beings, yet the two of them would argue fiercely about religion.

The teacher believed in the very letter of the Bible and in hell-fire, whereas Hans Christian believed with all his heart in his mother's teaching that God was love.

They argued about other matters, also, while ideas fairly set their brains on fire. Mr. Muller kindled in his pupil's heart a flame for learning. Hans Christian made great gains in his studies.

Although he was now free from Meisling, the rector had brought about a lasting change in Hans Christian's personality. He had made fun of his pupil's open and sensitive nature and the excitable feelings that rose in him. Now Hans Christian tried to appear quite different from the person he had been.

He himself made fun of any expression of feeling, and thought that he had rid himself of it, and yet he would be miserable for a whole day if someone frowned upon him.

The few poems he wrote at this time were humorous. Formerly he had written only tragedies. A complete change had come over him. It was as though a stunted plant had been transplanted and was sending out new shoots.

The Wulffs' oldest daughter, Henrietta, a clever girl, liked him and encouraged his humor. She was a girl to whom he could tell his innermost thoughts. She understood him and was like a sister to him. Perhaps because she was a hunchback, she was sensitive to his feelings of not being as good-looking as other young men.

She encouraged him to send his poem, "The Dying Child," around to newspapers. It was finally published. Then the well-known poet Heiberg, who was kind to him, accepted two of his humorous poems and published them in his newspaper, the *Flying Post*. The poems were signed only with the letter *H*.

The evening the *Flying Post* appeared with his poems, Hans Christian was having supper with the Wulffs. The captain and his wife did not think highly of his talent as a poet. Hans Christian told only Henrietta that the poems would be in the newspaper that night.

Captain Wulff came in with the paper in his hand. "This evening," he said, "there are two excellent poems in the newspaper. They are by Heiberg, although he signs only his initial. Nobody else could write anything like them."

Hans Christian's heart leaped with delight.

Henrietta giggled, then cried out, "Hans Christian wrote them!"

The young poet expected praise, but Captain Wulff and his wife were silent. All of the pleasure of having his poems appear in print drained from Hans Christian. Deeply hurt, he picked up his hat and left without eating.

He was very unhappy when he climbed to his tiny garret room. He lighted his candle, then went to lean on the windowsill and stare out at the moon. It shone on the roof tops, casting weird shadows from the chimneys. Often he stood there staring out of his narrow window and imagining himself traveling in far lands.

Tonight he was too unhappy for his imaginary journeys. Then as he thought about the matter, he began to see the Wulffs' point of view. No doubt they thought he had been writing poems when he should have been studying. They had always tried to impress upon him that his first duty was to study, study, study.

The examinations he must take to enter the Copenhagen University were not far off.

He sighed and turned away from the window. Then he sat down and opened a schoolbook. But when he later blew out his candle upon going to bed, he took to sleep with him the knowledge that Captain Wulff had for a time believed that his poems were written by the great Heiberg.

Panic seized Hans Christian with the approach of his examinations. He was sure that he would not pass.

When he next went to Counsellor Collin's house for dinner, the man looked grave and asked his ward how he was doing.

Hans Christian replied that he was working hard but that he feared he might not pass.

"If you fail," Mr. Collin told him, "it will be the end. I can't ask the king for any more help for you."

Hans Christian gulped, and he felt a tightening of his stomach muscles. "I will try my best to pass," he promised.

Now he did not waste time staring at the moon and dreaming of traveling. His candle burned low as he studied late into the night.

One evening as he was having dinner at the home of Orsted the critic, he met a young man named Von Schmidten. The stranger seemed shy and quiet. Hans Christian thought he had just arrived from the country, and feeling very much the city person, he tried to put the young man at ease.

"Are you going up for the examinations this year?" he asked.

"Yes," Von Schmidten said. "I am."

"I am, too," Hans Christian said with a trace of pride. He jabbered on of his hopes and ambitions and, of course, mentioned the poems he had written. "When Captain Wulff read them, he thought Heiberg had written them," he said.

When he went to the Copenhagen University for the examinations, Hans Christian found that Von Schmidten, whom he had taken for a country bumpkin, was a well-known professor who would examine him in mathematics.

Hans Christian was embarrassed, but the

professor was kind and said to him, "What is the first poetical work you will give us when you have finished the examinations?"

"I don't know, sir," he replied. "But please do not give me too hard questions in mathematics."

"Then you know something about the subject?"

"I did when I came, but now all that I know has left my mind, I'm afraid."

However, he passed. He had proved to the king and the others who had helped him that he had ability and the willpower to work hard.

Mr. Muller, his tutor, lived on the other side of the city, and every day on his long walk Hans Christian made up poems and tales in his head, as he had done as a boy under his mother's gooseberry bush.

Now that the strain of the examinations was over, the ideas that had been at work in his brain "flew like a swarm of bees out into the world."

He decided to write a book about what he

had seen during his walks across the city. He wrote for long hours every day, hardly taking time to eat except when he went out to dinner. His friends did not especially approve of his writing a book, but since he had worked hard, they decided that he should be allowed to do as he pleased. This was his vacation.

Before his vacation was over, he had finished *A Journey on Foot from the Holm Canal to the East Point of Amack.* In it he displayed that he had a "seeing eye" and a fine poetic fancy. It showed his habit of joking about his own feelings.

Parts of the manuscript were published in the *Flying Post.* It was gay and fresh and readers liked it. He had to publish the book at his own expense. This he did by going among his friends and getting subscriptions to buy the book. The first edition sold out to subscribers. The critics were kind, and a publisher offered to bring out a second edition at his own expense.

The book did fairly well. Hans Christian

proudly took the money he earned from it to Mr. Collin to bank for him.

Then he wrote a short play making fun of the old tragedies he had formerly written. It was accepted and enjoyed a short run at the Royal Theater. It was here that he had struggled as a penniless boy to become a ballet dancer and singer. It was on this very stage that he had knelt one New Year's Day and recited the Lord's Prayer.

He stood behind the scenes sweating with worry as the play was being acted.

Afterwards he ran all the way to the Collin house and threw himself into a chair, weeping.

Madame Collin tried to comfort him. "Don't cry," she said sensibly. "Famous authors, even Adam Oehlenschlager, were often hissed."

"But they didn't hiss," Hans Christian sobbed. "They applauded. They cried, 'Long live Andersen!'"

"Oh!" she said. "Then you are crying for happiness. I am so glad."

CHAPTER 11

First Love

Andersen worked hard and was successful as a student at Copenhagen University. He passed his final examinations with highest marks. Now he felt that he had put his boyhood behind him. And he knew what he wanted to do. He would win fame as a writer.

His grant from the king was finished, and

he must now make his living. With the royalties he got from *A Journey on Foot* he moved from his little garret to what he called "a heavenly blue room" in a better part of town.

At Christmas he brought out a collection of his poems. One of his good friends, Mrs. Ingemann, wrote about her favorites of the poems, "The little elves of our childhood seem to me to be, on the whole, your good geniuses. . . . I am sure the elves will show you the right way."

Andersen longed to hear himself spoken of as the greatest poet in the world, but the critics did not pay much attention to his collection. Annoyed, he decided to write a novel that would at once make him rich and famous. At first he thought that he would write about Jutland, for that was one of the places he had dreamed of visiting as he leaned on the windowsill of his garret room and stared at the moon. But he did not know anything about Jutland except that it was a peninsula, part of Denmark, and a region of marshes and heaths. Then he decided to write a historical novel about Odense. There was a place he knew well.

In the summer of 1830 he went there to visit. He was saddened to see his mother in the poorhouse, her mind failing.

Madame Iversen, the widow of the printer, asked him to stay at her house. There, however, he did not find time for writing, or even time to think about the book he hoped to write. Madame Iversen had several grand-daughters visiting her. They were gay and fun-loving, and much of the time was spent in picnicking.

He longed to fall in love with one of these charming girls. However, he could feel nothing for any of them but comradeship.

One of his friends, Christian Voight, invited Andersen to visit at his home in Faaborg, a pleasant town on the sea. Christian introduced him to his sister, Riborg. At first Andersen thought her rather plain, with her dark skin and brown eyes and hair. Later, when they happened to be alone together in the parlor, he talked to her about the book he planned to write.

Her dark eyes came alive with interest. He felt that she understood him completely.

The next day they went sailing and had a picnic on a beautiful island. Riborg made a wreath of oak leaves. Then she shyly handed it to her brother to place on Andersen's head.

There was a picnic every day and one night a dance. Andersen, who by this time knew how awkward he was as a dancer, stood leaning against the wall, feeling very left out of things.

Riborg came over. "Let's sit and talk," she said.

He found her the wisest young woman he

had ever talked with. Hers was not the light, amusing chatter of Madame Iversen's granddaughters. She had a wide knowledge of music, poetry, and books. Best of all, she had read *A Journey on Foot* and liked it. Naturally he told her of his hopes and ambitions, and she listened with grave understanding.

When the party ended, Andersen's heart was beating fast, and his head was in a whirl. The world had suddenly become warm and glowing. This was what he had been searching for — the woman of his dreams — the one who was in tune with him. With her by his side to inspire him, he would write wonderful things. Life would be a lovely song.

The next morning at the breakfast table he saw Christian give him a strange look, and then he realized that he had been staring at Riborg. No doubt the love that was in his heart showed in his eyes.

After the meal was over, Christian beckoned to his friend to follow him into the study. "I see how it is with you," he said. "Don't get in any deeper. Riborg is engaged to the son of the druggist. They would be married by this time if my parents had not objected to him."

On the last day of his visit Andersen and Riborg walked in the garden. "I am going to name the heroine of my next book for you, if you will allow me to," he said shyly.

"I would like that very much." She blushed. Then, "Would you write me a poem?" she asked.

He stopped in the walk and gave her a long look. Then he took a scrap of paper and a pencil from his pocket and wrote:

You have become my thinking's single thought,
My heart's first love; it had no love before.
I love you as no love on earth is wrought,
I love you now and love you evermore.

She read the poem, then read it again. "Do — do you mean this?" she asked.

"I really do."

"But — but I'm not free. . . ."

"Yes, I know. Christian told me."

Then he took her arm. "Do you really love this other man?"

Her head drooped. She did not answer.

"If you do, I will pray God that He make fortune smile upon you. But if you are not sure, don't make me unhappy. With your help I can become anything. I'll work. I'll do everything you and your parents desire of me."

"I am promised," she said in a small voice.

He seized her hands and pressed them. "Farewell, then! Farewell — perhaps forever!"

She burst into tears.

That afternoon as he was leaving the house, she pressed a note into his hand.

He got into the coach, and as it set out, he saw her sweet face smiling at him from a window of the house. He felt that he was leaving his heart behind with her.

He opened the note and read, "Farewell, farewell! I hope that Christian will soon be able to tell me that you once again are as happy and calm as you were before."

As the coach rolled along, he thought of his shattered dreams. What had he been thinking of? What had he to offer a well-born young woman like Riborg? He had seen the druggist's store with its bustling business. He had seen the fine home of the druggist's son, whom Riborg was to marry. He, Hans Christian Andersen, lived in a shabby room. He had only a small amount of money earned from *A Journey on Foot*. His future was dim.

Back in Copenhagen he started to work on his novel. But ideas would not come. He started an opera, then wrote new poems which he read to whoever would listen. They were written with Riborg in mind. Among them was a poem called "Two Brown Eyes."

People who heard his poems guessed his secret — that he was in love. This he denied, but his friends still teased him.

He brought out his second book of poems. The critics were not kind about it. Andersen was plunged into still deeper despair.

The Collins, his good friends, were still watching over him. Counsellor Collin called Andersen into his study. "Why don't you take some of your savings and go on a little journey?" he suggested. "You need a change. You need a new outlook on life. A trip will give you fresh ideas. You will come back ready to work."

At once Andersen knew that this was what he wanted to do.

CHAPTER 12

"A Mermaid Has No Tears"

It was the spring of 1831 when Andersen first left Denmark. He was twenty-six. He went no farther than Germany, but it was a foreign land. Here every experience was new. Here fresh scenes made him forget the ache that was in his heart. Everything amazed him and filled his mind so that he forgot that only a short time ago he had thought that he could never be happy again.

123

He saw mountains for the first time and was awed by their beauty. He took a long walking trip. He had nothing to do but to look, to live, to enjoy. No one was better fitted than Hans Christian Andersen to make the most of such an experience.

Armed with letters of introduction his friends had given him, he called upon several writers. They treated him with kindness and loaned him books by the most famous German writers. At night in his room he read them until he fell asleep.

In six weeks he went back to Copenhagen and at once started to write a book about his experiences. Henrietta Wulff said, "It would take *you,* dear Andersen, to write a travel book after only six weeks abroad." She often took it upon herself to prick his little bubbles of vanity.

"You forget," he reminded her gently, "that my first book was made out of a walking trip across this very city. Most people who have lived here for years did not know what was under their noses."

"You are right," she said. "You do have a seeing eye and a mind that soaks up impressions. No doubt you saw more in six weeks than most of us would have in that many months."

Travel Silhouettes was the title of his little travel book. In it were clear-cut scenes, impressions, poems, even a short but charming fairy tale. The book made a small splash in the literary world.

For two years he wrote poems and from them earned a small amount of money. He also adapted plays from foreign books. These he took to the Royal Theater, but they were always sent back.

He was becoming desperate. The pressure of trying to write to make a living caused him to write too fast.

He did not need much money. He had grown used to very little food. Many of his meals were only cheese and crackers. His friends still invited him often to dinner. But his room had to be paid for and his clothes had to be kept neat and clean.

In every letter he got from his mother she begged for money. He sent her all that he could spare. Then he received a message from Colonel Guldberg telling him that her mind had failed and that she had been put in an asylum.

Andersen knew that most of the money he sent her had gone for the brandy which she had learned to crave to deaden the pain in her legs, pain she had gotten from standing in the cold stream to do people's washings.

He went at once to Odense. His mother did not know him. Her clothes were untidy, her gray hair was uncombed — she who had taught him neatness and cleanliness. His heart ached at the sight.

He stayed with Colonel Guldberg. His old friends were kind to him and praised his travel books and poems. But his heart remained like lead.

Unable to do anything for his mother, he returned to Copenhagen. Here he had to face up to his problems: poverty and the ghost of failure.

In his heart he knew that he was a genius.
But no one else believed that he was one.
And after all, what had he done to prove it?
Yet he *must* be a genius. Otherwise he
was a dreamer like his unhappy father — or
perhaps . . . could he perhaps hold in his
brain the seed of madness like his grandfather?

Pushed into action by this thought, he
picked up his pen, only to stare at the blank
piece of paper in front of him.

The Collins were still his family. Counsellor Collin had turned his problem child,
Andersen, over to his son Edvard. Edvard
was a law student and quite proper. He took
his duty of guiding his friend very seriously.

Andersen longed for a closer friendship
with the young man he worshipped as an
idol. Edvard was very fond of Andersen, but
he held him somewhat at arm's length. And
he was often embarrassed by his friend's habit
of always reading aloud his poems at every
gathering.

Edvard knew that often people asked

Andersen to read aloud only to giggle at him. At one party Edvard said, "If you read aloud tonight, I shall leave."

Of course Andersen was asked to read, and read he did. He saw Edvard scowling at him, but young Collin did not leave, and Andersen read with such feeling that people did not laugh, but were moved by his performance.

Andersen would always regard Counsellor Collin as his father and the Collin house as his only home. Edvard would always be his dearest friend, even though the young law student considered it his duty to try to improve him.

"Don't always let your feelings be on such a seesaw," Edvard said. "You are either way up or way down."

"Oh!" Andersen exclaimed. "I wish I could be solid like you. But then I would miss those moments of great joy I sometimes know. I must be as I am, dear Edvard. Do not find so much fault with me."

He had thought he had returned from

128

Germany cured of the Riborg affair. Yet there was in his heart still a great longing — if not for Riborg herself, for someone who would understand.

When he had first come to the Collin house, Andersen had made up stories for Louise, the youngest of the children, and had cut out paper figures for her. Now, almost overnight, she had turned into a young lady. She was not really beautiful, but she had large blue eyes and a sweet smile.

He found her a kind and understanding companion. When he was with her he felt completely at peace and happy. He began spending more and more time at the Collins' home so that he could be with her. Then he knew that a strange feeling was creeping into his heart once more. He had written for Riborg a poem about brown eyes. Now he wrote a poem about blue eyes.

"It is a beautiful little poem," Louise said, but she did not seem to take it personally.

The Collins went to spend the summer at their country place.

"May I write to you?" Andersen asked Louise.

"I'd love to hear from you," she replied.

The letters flew from his little room to Louise. On paper he told her the things he could not say to her face. He poured his heart out.

Louise was alarmed. She confided to her married sister, Ingeborg, that in showing their friend sympathy and understanding, she had awakened his love. She cared for him only as a brother. She would not consider marriage to one so flighty in his emotions. She wanted someone solid like herself.

Ingeborg advised her sister to let Andersen know that from now on she must show all of his letters to her, Ingeborg.

Andersen's letters became fewer, and he did not pour out his inner feelings so freely. He did write of his loneliness, his need for understanding.

When the Collins returned to Copenhagen, Andersen found it impossible to see Louise alone. She was always with members of her family. She was at the time falling in love with a young man as solid as she.

She told Andersen nothing of what was going on. Neither did the other members of the family. So it came as a shock to him when her engagement was announced at a New Year's party in 1833.

Andersen was stunned. Here was failure once more. He was hurt, too, by the fact that no one in the family had told him. It made him feel shut out. They did not consider him as one of themselves after all. For once, he did not cry. Later he would write in one of his stories, "A mermaid has no tears and so she suffers all the more." This time he could not find relief from his pain in weeping.

CHAPTER 13

The Magic of Travel

Once more Andersen was in the depths of despair. He longed to go away where no one knew him. Counsellor Collin sensed what was going on in his young friend's heart.

He said, "I believe that the king might accept your petition for a year's travel expenses if you take him one of your latest books."

Andersen's heart leaped at the idea. Then he became more thoughtful and said, "It seems very rude to ask a favor at the same time I make a gift."

"That's the way it must be done," Mr. Collin said. "I'll ask the king for an audience."

Andersen was shaking with nervousness when he went before King Frederick the Sixth. He bowed low, then held out his book.

"What's the book about?" the king said gruffly.

"It — it's poems about Denmark."

"So? Well, where is your petition?"

Andersen gave it to the king. "It seems to me dreadful to ask a favor at the same time I make a gift," he said. "But they tell me that is the only way to do it."

The king laughed at Andersen's awkward shyness and lost his gruffness. He granted the petition — for two years of travel instead of one.

All of the Collins went to the ship to see Andersen off for Italy. "You will come back brimming with ideas," Mr. Collin told him.

"Some day," Andersen said seriously, "I

will bring honor to you whom I love so well."

Edvard handed him a letter. "Read it when you are at sea," he said.

Andersen would reread that letter many times, for it said more than the distant Edvard had ever told him face to face:

Monday noon, April 22, 1833

Dear Friend,

Suddenly the idea struck me that it might please you to receive a letter from me before you reached Hamburg and before you could expect a letter. Believe me, I'm intensely sorry at your departure. I shall miss you dreadfully; I shall miss your coming up to my room to talk to me; on Tuesdays I'll miss you on your seat at the table. Still I know, you will miss more, for you are alone; but true, it is a consolation to know that one has friends back home who think of one, so you have this consolation, for we shall constantly remember you with love. Goodbye, my dear, dear friend! God let us meet again glad and happy in two years.

Edvard

This was the last letter he would get from
anyone for many weeks. He flooded his
friends with lively descriptions of the places
he visited. In Paris he joined a group of
other Danish travelers and with them took
sight-seeing trips and visited cafes and the-
aters. He kept an album with autographs
and his own clever pen-and-ink sketches.
Today the Royal Library in Copenhagen
proudly displays that album.

A new poem was beginning to form in his
mind. It was based on an old Danish folk
song, "Agnete and the Merman." His grandmother had sung it to him as a child, and the
story it told of the earth and the sea had remained with him. One day this story would
blossom into Andersen's lovely fairy tale
"The Little Mermaid," but first it would take
form as a poem.

He started to write "Agnete" while he was
still in Paris. He would show his critics that
he did have genius. They would see how
travel had caused his powers to develop. He
wrote at white heat.

Life in Paris was too lively for him to stay with his work. He was invited to visit friends in a quiet town in the Jura Mountains of Switzerland. "You will find peace and quiet there," he was told. "It is the perfect place for a writer."

His new home was in the watch-making town of Le Locle. It was in a valley high in the mountains, and often fluffy clouds floated below them. There was peace and quiet among the dark pine trees. The houses were white, and the yards were spotlessly clean. In the windows of each house was a display of watches. Here and there were pretty dark bushes with red berries which somehow re-

minded him of pictures in his childhood
A B C book and of his old home in Odense.

He finished "Agnete" in about two weeks
and sent the poem off to Edvard. Then he
set out happily for Italy. He was sure that
his friends in Denmark would be pleased
with his new work. As the stage rolled toward Italy there was a song in his heart. The
beauty of Italy was almost more than he

could bear. There his heart seemed to expand with the joy of living until he thought it about to burst.

Some day those impressions would come through in his story of "Thumbelisa," in which a tiny girl, seated on a swallow's back, is borne away to the warm countries:

> . . . and then the swallow flew away, high up in the air . . . above the biggest mountains where the snow never melts; and Thumbelisa shivered in the cold air, but then she crept under the bird's warm feathers, and only stuck out her little head to look at the beautiful sights beneath it.
>
> Then at last they reached the warm countries. The sun shone with a warmer glow than here; the sky was twice as high, and the most beautiful green and blue grapes grew in clusters on the banks and hedgerows. Oranges and lemons hung in the woods which were fragrant with myrtles and sweet herbs, and beautiful children ran about the roads playing with the large gorgeously-colored butterflies.

Andersen's happiness faded when he

reached Milan and found a letter from Edvard. He did not like the poem; neither did
anyone else. No publisher would take it. He
was trying to have it printed by public sub-
scription, but few wanted to subscribe. "Give
up writing," Edvard suggested. "You will
never make a living at it."

Andersen wrote back, " 'Agnete' and my
stay in Le Locle close one portion of my
poetic life." But he said nothing about giv-
ing up writing.

Then he got a letter from Mr. Collin telling him that his mother had died. At first he
was grateful that her poverty and misery were
at an end. Then a great sense of loneliness
swept over him. Now there was no one on
earth who belonged to him.

Everyone that he knew had someone — a
father or mother, a wife and children, brothers and sisters. Only he was completely alone.

But Andersen could not remain unhappy
for long in Italy. In Florence, it seemed to
him that his mind and soul were expanding.
There he gazed by the hour at wonderful

masterpieces of painting and sculpture. He wrote to friends:

> The marble looked into my soul. The snow melted away before my eyes and a new world of art opened. I wish I were just seventeen years old and had the same sentiments and ideas as now; I would surely become something; now I only see that I don't know anything, and life is so short; how can I possibly learn so enormously much? That is a sensation I have never known; it makes me intensely sad! My heart grows too big for me here in Italy, and yet it cannot hold all the splendor.

He left Italy knowing that he would never be the same again.

CHAPTER 14

First Fairy Tales

Andersen traveled slowly to Germany. He did not want to go home, but his money was running out. He knew what was in store for him there — more criticism, more advice.

Yet there was excitement bubbling in his brain. A new book was struggling to be born. This time it would be a novel. Counsellor Collin had begged him not to write a travel book. "Too many good ones have been written," he had said. This would not be a travel book, yet its setting would be Italy. The story would be about himself. He had been called an improviser, one who recites or sings in verse, making up the words as he goes along. He called his novel *The Improvisatore*.

His first evening in Copenhagen he hurried to the Collins' home. It happened to be Louise's birthday, so there was cause for a double celebration. Even old Mr. Collin had tears in his eyes when he greeted Hans Christian. Andersen felt that no member of the family could have been treated with more affection.

He rented a small room on the sunless side of a house because it was cheaper. For a time he put aside most of his letter writing and visiting, and his novel poured forth from his pen onto paper.

When he had finished, he dedicated the book: "To the Conference Counsellor Collin and his noble wife, in whom I found parents, whose children were my brothers and sisters, whose home was my home, I present the best that I possess."

At that time it was not only the best, but the only thing he possessed. He even owed for his last month's room rent.

He gave the book to Edvard to take to a publisher. Edward was offered only twenty pounds for it.

"Take it," Hans Christian said. "I must pay my room rent, and my friends will get tired of feeding me."

He did not speak of how shabby his clothes were, or the fact that his shoes were split.

While waiting for his book to be published, he dashed off four fairy tales for children. He tried them because he was in such great need of money. They were "The Tinder Box," "Little Claus and Big Claus," "Little Ida's Flowers," and "The Princess and the Pea."

As was his habit he gave the tales to friends to read. As he handed the stories to Henrietta Wulff, he said with a laugh, "Orsted the critic says that if *The Improvisatore* will make me famous, these will make me immortal. He says they are the most perfect

143

things I have written. But I don't believe it; he doesn't know Italy."

Andersen called his fairy tales "those trifles." They, too, were about himself and the people he knew. At the time he wrote them he was desperate. "Little Claus and Big Claus" and "The Tinder Box" were about magic ways of making money. They were born of his own daydreams.

Here was something new in storytelling. The tales were written for children, but they delighted grown-ups as well. Adults found in them a deep inner meaning. They were gems which would endure through the years.

At last *The Improvisatore* came out. Andersen clasped a copy to his chest. "This is the book that will make me famous," he said.

He gave autographed copies to all of his friends at whose houses he had eaten dinner so many times. They all praised the book. And the critics also said kind things about its freshness and its aliveness.

It ran into several editions and was translated into a number of foreign languages.

Elated, Hans Christian plunged into another novel, *O.T.* Before it was published, he had started another.

"I shall be the best novelist in Denmark," he told Edvard.

"My modest friend," Edvard said dryly.

Andersen thought of his novels as his most important work, but fairy tales still nagged at his mind and demanded to be written. How well he knew the source of his inspiration is shown in one of these tales, "The Pen and the Inkpot":

In the room of a poet, where his inkstand stood upon the table, it was said, "It is wonderful what can come out of an inkstand, and what will the next thing be? It is wonderful!"

"Yes, certainly," said the inkstand. "It's extraordinary, that's what I always say," he exclaimed to the pen and other things on the table that were near enough to hear. "It is wonderful what a number of these things can come out of me. It's quite incredible and I really don't know myself what will be the next thing when that man begins to dip into me.

One drop out of me is enough for a half page of paper; and what cannot be contained in one half page? . . . I assure you that I don't think of anything."

"There you are right," said the pen. "You don't think at all; if you did you would know that you only supply the fluid. You give the fluid that I may show upon the paper what dwells in me and what I would bring to the day. It is the pen that writes . . ."

. . . .

And each of them felt a belief that he had answered well; and it was a pleasing belief to feel that one has given a good answer . . . and accordingly they slept upon it. But the poet did not sleep. Thoughts welled up within him, like tones from a violin, falling like pearls, rushing like the storm wind through the forests. He understood his own heart in these thoughts and caught a ray from the Eternal Master.

To Him be all the honor.

CHAPTER 15

The Turning
Point

The publication of *The Improvisatore* marked a turning point in Hans Christian Andersen's life. At last he was looked up to and respected. Those who had laughed at him before were now glad to shake his hand.

In these happy days he remembered that seventeen years ago as a penniless boy in Copenhagen he had walked along the harbor thinking of begging the captain of some ship to allow him to work his passage back to Odense.

Now in January, 1836, he was able to rent two rooms. From his study window he could see the harbor where he had once stood in such deep despair.

It was snowing and cold outside, but in his study a cheery fire crackled in the stove. He wrote to a friend, "I think of the poor boy in Odense who wore wooden shoes, and my heart softens, and I bless the good Lord. . . . No winter has been so quiet and blissful."

His novel *O.T.* was published and, although it had been carelessly written, it was fairly well received. Meantime, he had been writing more fairy tales. It bothered him that he was not looked upon as the best novelist in Denmark. Yet everywhere he went people stared at him and he was spoken of as "the man who writes those charming fairy tales."

He easily stood out in any crowd. He was

still ugly, with his long nose and close-set eyes. Yet there was an attractiveness about him, and his smile lighted up his plain features. Now that he was able to dress well, he did so. He wanted to forget forever the secondhand clothes which he had had to fill out with theater programs. He wanted to forget the wooden shoes. His clothes were of fine quality; he wore a high hat.

Since he had not won the fame he longed for with his novels, he decided to write another drama for the theater. It was finally accepted after he was kept waiting for many weeks for a decision.

He was invited to read his drama, "The Mulatto," before the king and queen. They praised his work and were very kind to him.

At last the time came for the first performance of the play. The night before, Andersen had been so excited that he was unable to close his eyes. The brightly colored playbills were posted on the walls. He had walked back and forth in front of the theater to look at them and thrill with pride.

On opening night, when he came riding in style in a cab to the theater, he was delighted to see crowds of people there waiting to buy tickets.

Then guns boomed and royal messengers

rode through the streets with the message that King Frederick the Sixth had died that morning.

The theater doors of course were not opened that night. They remained closed for two months. During that time Andersen was in a state of suspense and excitement. He could not work. At last, under King Christian the Eighth, the theater reopened. "The Mulatto" was a success. Now Andersen could relax and breathe more freely.

His drama was given in several Danish and Swedish cities and towns. Then he was invited by some students of Lund to visit that old Swedish town. A public dinner was given in his honor, and speeches were made praising him.

He was staying the night with a family of the town.

"A group of students is coming to serenade you," his host told him.

Andersen's heart began to pound. He had not expected anything like this. He stood by the big front window. The students in their blue caps came swinging along arm in arm.

He went outside to meet them, feeling unworthy of such homage. The students removed their caps. It was all that Andersen could do to hold back his tears.

The students gave a loud "Hurray!" and held their caps up high.

One of them stepped before him and gave a short speech. The words would be engraved upon Andersen's memory all his life: "When your native land and the nations of Europe offer their homage, then may you never forget that the first public honors were conferred upon you by the students of Lund."

Andersen managed to reply, "I must now earn a name to make myself worthy of the honor you have done me."

He pressed the hands of those near him, then rushed off to his room to give way to tears of joy.

When he returned to Copenhagen, he found himself often the guest of the best families of the country. He was given a place in the court stalls of the theater where royalty sat. This was an honor given only to famous writers.

Every evening he went to the theater. It was like a club to him. As he sat among the great of the land, he remembered when he had been a gangling boy at the back of the stage.

In the summer he was a guest at several rich country homes. Here he enjoyed walking in the woods or sitting beside a stream watching wild game or the storks striding along on long red legs.

Here in the peaceful country he wrote many of his fairy tales. He was puzzled and a bit annoyed by their popularity. He wrote them for children, but it became the style for his books of fairy tales to be on the tables of adults.

Although the idea for "The Ugly Duckling" had been planted in his mind long before this time, it was while he was a guest at the beautiful country manors that he found the background for this tale:

The country was lovely just then; it was summer. The wheat was golden and the oats still green; the hay was stacked in the rich low-lying meadows, where the stork was marching about on his long red legs, chattering Egyptian, the language his mother had taught him.

Roundabout field and meadow lay great woods in the midst of which were deep lakes. Yes, the country certainly was delicious. In the sunniest spot stood an old mansion surrounded by a deep moat, and great dock leaves grew from the walls of the house right down to the water's edge; some of them were so tall that a small child could stand upright under them. In amongst the leaves it was as secluded as in the depths of a forest; and there a duck was sitting on her nest.

CHAPTER 16

Jenny Lind

At this time in his life Andersen met a person who would be of greatest importance to him. In 1840 he was living in a good hotel. One day he happened to glance down at the register and saw the name *Jenny Lind*. He knew that she was the best singer in Sweden. He decided that it would be a friendly act if he called upon her.

She was polite, but he thought her rather

cool and plain. She told him that she was in Copenhagen for only a few days. She and her father had come there to see the city.

He quickly forgot her.

Three years later she came back to Copenhagen. One of Andersen's friends, the ballet master of the Royal Theater, knew Jenny Lind.

The ballet master went to Andersen and told him that Miss Lind had spoken of him. She remembered him very kindly and had now read his books.

"She asked for you to come to see her," the ballet master said. "If you do, beg her to sing upon the stage of the Royal Theater. You will be most enchanted by what you hear."

Andersen went, and this time Jenny Lind greeted him warmly, extending her hand and praising his writings. "I adore your fairy tales," she said.

There it was again — always the fairy tales! He could not understand what magic there was in them.

The conversation soon turned to her singing at the theater.

"Oh, no!" she cried. "I have never sung outside of Sweden. Everyone in my native land loves me. They are kind to me because I am one of them. If I should sing in Copenhagen and should be hissed . . . I dare not venture it."

"I am sure," Andersen told her, "that you would find the Copenhagen audiences as kind as those in Sweden."

Finally, after much coaxing, she agreed to take a singing part in an opera. Andersen wrote of the event as the greatest enjoyment the citizens of Copenhagen had ever had. In his autobiography, *The Story of My Life,* he wrote pages raving about her. "The whole of Copenhagen was in raptures," he said.

Andersen loved to travel, and travel he did, to Germany, to England, to Sweden, to Italy again.

Everywhere he went he was received by the highest in the land. Yet he liked to wander about the streets of the poorer quarters. He felt strangely drawn to the unfortunates in every land where he traveled.

One day he saw in the slums of London a thin little girl holding out some matches to sell. He stooped over to buy them from her. His kind smile lighted up his face. Shyly she curtsied. As he walked on, he thought about her. Then the memory came to him of his grandmother's telling him of how her parents had sent her out to beg. She was too shy and hid under a bridge. When he went back to his room, he started to write "The Little Match Girl."

There would always be in him something of the child. From experience he knew the whole range of emotions from black despair to wildest joy. No one could read his tales without feeling his own depths of feeling. He brought everything to life — matches, tin soldiers, flowers, and people. Therein lies their magic.

When Andersen was visiting in London,

his hostess, Lady Blessingdon, got a letter from the writer Charles Dickens. "I must meet Andersen," he wrote. "I shall go to London especially to meet him."

Andersen was in Lady Blessingdon's study when a tall man with a handsome face and wavy hair was shown in. Andersen leaped to his feet and rushed forward. He recognized Dickens from his pictures. They clasped hands and gazed at each other happily. "I knew it would be like this!" Hans Christian cried. "We are kindred spirits!"

They had a good talk and Dickens invited Andersen to visit him and his family at his home. Andersen went, and it was a visit he would treasure in his memory.

It pleased his vanity to be able to send back to Edvard a clipping from an English paper. It called him, Andersen, "one of the most remarkable and interesting men of this day."

Upon his return to Denmark he wrote a volume of short stories called *A Christmas Greeting to My English Friends*. It bore a dedication to Charles Dickens.

One day when Andersen was out walking, he saw coming toward him a fat man dressed in shabby clothes. There was something familiar about him. Then a horrible memory rushed over Andersen. He heard a harsh voice shouting, "You are stupid, crude! Your writings will be trampled under foot in the print shop. You will end in an insane asylum!" It was Meisling, the tormenter of his student days.

The shabby man held out his hand. "Forgive me for being so cruel to you," he said. "I am ashamed. You have become great."

The ever-ready tears rushed to Andersen's eyes. He clasped Meisling's hand. This man had hurt him more than any other person ever had. He had caused scars which would never heal, but Andersen promptly forgave him.

CHAPTER 17

Rare Honors

Andersen had enjoyed a measure of success. Yet it was not enough to give him a feeling of security. He was the kind of person who would always be on a seesaw of emotions. He could be either wild with joy over seeing a beautiful tree in leaf in the spring, or deep in despair over some criticism of his work.

He envied steady people like the Collins

who did not suffer from changing moods the way he did. In spite of his fame he was still worried about where to get the money to pay his rent and pay for his food.

Edvard Collin had married and now all of Andersen's friends seemed happy in their homes. Only Hans Christian Andersen had no wife. But what good was it to think of getting married? He was having trouble earning his own living.

Then one day as he sat in his study wondering what was to become of him, there came a knock at the door. It was as though a good fairy had read the message in his heart. A handsome man introduced himself as Count Conrad Rantzau-Breitenburg. "I am a member of the commission to aid authors," he said, seating himself and looking around the bare room. "I read *The Improvisatore* with a great deal of pleasure. Is there anything I can do for you?"

Andersen gasped. For a moment he was at a loss to know what the count meant.

The count went on, "As you no doubt

know, Denmark sets aside a pension fund for writers and musicians whose work shows promise."

Andersen managed to say that although he thought his claims as a writer were still modest, he would greatly appreciate some state support.

Soon after the count's call, Andersen was granted a pension of two hundred rix-dollars a year. Although it was not much, it was enough for his frugal way of living. Best of all, it was a steady amount. He wrote gaily in his dairy, "Now I have a little breadfruit tree in my garden. I need no longer sing for crumbs." The pressure of having to write in order to eat was removed.

He published *A Picture Book Without Pictures* and his fourth collection of tales, which included "The Daisy," "The Wild Swans," and "The Steadfast Tin Soldier."

Then he took another trip abroad, this time doing much of his traveling on trains instead of stagecoaches. He was much excited by this new method of travel and wrote about his sensations in detail in the travel book that came out of this journey, *Poet's Bazaar*.

Everywhere he went he was received by royalty, and honors and gifts were heaped upon him. Once he was invited to visit the summer home of King Christian. While he was dining with the family, he glanced slyly at the king, wondering whether he remembered that when he was Prince Christian he had given Hans Christian an audience and advised him to be sensible and become a cabinetmaker.

People had laughed at Andersen behind his back when he insisted upon reading his writings aloud. Now it was considered an event when he gave one of his readings after dinner. Candles were placed beside him. The room was hushed and the listeners were caught up in the magic of the tale.

Even his looks seemed to have changed. Once he had been ugly, but now his fine character showed through and his face had taken on dignity and nobility.

Like him, Jenny Lind was becoming a

world-wide sensation. Their paths seldom crossed, but he thought about her much of the time.

He heard that Jenny Lind was in Germany. He went there hoping to spend Christmas with her, but although he had written her that he was coming, she did not invite him to see her. He sat all day in his lonely hotel room and felt sorry for himself.

At last they met at a social gathering, and he told her of his loneliness at Christmas. "But I thought of course you were spending your time with princes and princesses," she said.

She then invited him to spend New Year's Eve with her. She lighted the Christmas tree and sang for him. Later that evening he tried to tell her what was in his heart, but she said, "I love you as a brother. There can be nothing else between us."

Brokenhearted he went to his room. He had really known from the first that nothing could come of his feeling for her. But she had had a deep effect upon his life and had

inspired many of his fairy tales. He had her
in mind when he wrote in "The Little Mermaid":

> In the middle of the room was a broad stream
> of running water, and on this the mermaids
> and mermen danced to their own beautiful
> singing. No earthly beings have such lovely
> voices. The little mermaid sang more sweetly
> than any of them and they all applauded her.
> For a moment she felt glad at heart, for she
> knew that she had the finest voice either in
> the sea or on land.

He was thinking of her, too, in his story of
"The Nightingale":

> The nightingale sang delightfully, and the
> tears came into the emperor's eyes, nay, they
> rolled down his cheeks, and then the night-
> ingale sang more beautifully than ever; its
> notes touched all hearts. The emperor was
> charmed, and said the nightingale should have
> his gold slipper to wear round its neck. But
> the nightingale declined with thanks; it had
> been sufficiently rewarded.
>
> "I have seen tears in the eyes of the emperor;

that is my richest reward." . . . And then it again burst into its sweet heavenly song.

The years dashed by with great speed. Twice within ten years Hans Christian was torn with emotion when Denmark was at war with Prussia. He had a deep love for Germany, but his heart and soul belonged to Denmark.

By the time he was sixty, he was world-famous. Royalty of every country sent him gifts and decorations. He was at last free of want. His tales were published in many foreign countries. He kept on writing until there were 156 of them.

He still loved to travel. Through the years he had bought furniture he liked until he owned everything he needed except a bed.

"A bed would keep me chained down," he had said. "I want to feel free to go as I please." But at last he did buy a bed, one surprisingly small for such a tall man.

He made a face when he saw it in his room and sat down to write:

> I can see it will be my deathbed, because if it does not last as long as that it will not be worth the money! Oh, if I were only twenty once more I'd put an inkwell on my back, take two shirts and a pair of socks, tuck a quill pen at my side, and walk out into the wide world!

On December 6, 1867, a big festival was given in his honor in Odense. He was taken the night before to the home of the bishop, where he was to be a guest. He was so worked up with suspense, terror, and a toothache that he could not sleep.

"The schools are closed and the whole town is decorated in your honor," the bishop told him.

As Andersen got into a carriage to be driven to the Guild Hall, where the ceremony was to be held, he said to the bishop, "Now I know how it feels to be driven to one's execution."

It seemed like a dream to him to see the flags billowing, to see the crowds pushing to catch sight of him, to hear their hurrahs.

He was seated on the platform next to the burgomaster. The hall had been decorated with flags and flowers and a sculptured bust of Andersen. The burgomaster made a long speech. Andersen wished that his father and mother and grandmother were living to see him so honored. As the burgomaster spoke on and on, fleeting pictures passed through Andersen's mind — his mother with her skirts pinned up standing in cold water up to her knees, washing people's dirty clothes — his mad grandfather being chased through the streets — he himself being chased by boys who shouted, "There goes the playwright, crazy like his grandfather!"

At last the speech was ended. The burgomaster handed him a diploma naming him as the most honored citizen of Odense.

Andersen managed to keep from fainting or weeping as he made a brief "thank you" speech.

That night came the climax of the celebration. Nearly fifty years ago he had begged his mother to let him go to Copenhagen to seek his fortune. She had called in a fortune-teller who had said that he would become great and that some day all Odense would be lighted up for him.

The time had come. The bishop asked Andersen to step to the window. There he saw lanterns and candles shining from every window, and from all directions came parades of men carrying torches. The marchers

formed a square and sang for him. Then everyone broke into a cheer. He had been honored by kings and queens, but this was the high point of his life.

When the song was ended, the torches were thrown into the center of the square, making a bonfire. He saw kind faces all about him; he felt waves of warm love flowing to him. This was his home. Here he belonged. He went to bed still feeling that this was the climax of his life.

In the winter of 1872 he was taken with a cough which kept him in his room. The next summer his friends the Melchoirs took him to their country home. Here he was surrounded by the flowers he loved. Each day a fresh bouquet was placed in his room.

Andersen's seventieth birthday was a day rich in sunshine and blessings. Gifts and messages came to him from all directions. He was taken to the king's garden to see the statue showing him seated reading to a group of children. Friends had raised the money for this statue.

"It is a rare honor," he said, "to have a statue erected to one during his lifetime. But I wanted to be remembered as one who wrote for all people, not just for children."

The Melchoirs' home was a beautiful, peaceful place and here, as he became weaker and weaker, he was often visited by the king and the crown prince.

On the fourth of August, 1875, he drifted quietly out of life.

At his funeral service in Copenhagen, flowers were strewn up the aisle of the church. A great man had passed away, but he had left behind him something that would delight grown-ups and their children and their children's children as long as people would read.

Author's Note

Whan Hans Christian Andersen was an old man, he wrote: "Rich and serenely happy, my life is a beautiful fairy tale."

And it truly was like a fairy tale. But for a long time he was very poor. There was great unhappiness in his life, too, and his struggle for success was a long and hard one. Yet at the end of his life he was able to forget the poverty and unhappiness and bitter struggle, and remember only the good things that had happened to him.

The roots of his fairy tales are in his own life story. Most of the tales grew from things that happened to him as a boy. He wrote two autobiographies: *The Fairy Tale of My Life* and *The Story of My Life*. In them he tells nearly everything that happened to him.

When I was a child, I read and reread and

wept over Hans Christian Andersen's fairy tales. For a number of years now, I have been enjoying them over again in reading them to my grandchildren. It has been sheer pleasure to write about this man whose life was a fairy story.

I hope that the readers of this book will go back and read the most famous of his tales and that their pleasure in them will be made greater by knowing the life of this fine man.

Hans Christian Andersen wrote: "The story of my life is intended to teach the lesson it teaches me: that there is a loving God who arranges everything for the best."

SHANNON GARST

THE UGLY DUCKLING

The country was lovely just then; it was summer! The wheat was golden and the oats still green; the hay was stacked in the rich low-lying meadows, where the stork was marching about on his long red legs, chattering Egyptian, the language his mother had taught him.

Roundabout field and meadow lay great woods in the midst of which were deep lakes. Yes, the country certainly was delicious. In the sunniest spot stood an old mansion surrounded by a deep moat, and great dock leaves grew from the walls of the house right down to the water's edge; some of them were so tall that a small child could stand upright under them. In amongst the leaves it was as secluded as in the depths of a forest; and there a duck was sitting on her nest. Her little ducklings were just about to be hatched, but she was nearly tired of sitting, for it had lasted such a long time. Moreover, she had very few visitors, as the other ducks liked swimming about in the moat better than waddling up to sit under the dock leaves and gossip with her.

At last one egg after another began to crack. "Cheep, cheep!" they said. All the chicks had come to life, and were poking their heads out.

"Quack! quack!" said the duck; and then they all quacked their hardest, and looked about them on all sides among the green leaves; their mother allowed them to look as much as they liked, for green is good for the eyes.

"How big the world is to be sure!" said all the

young ones, for they certainly had ever so much more room to move about than when they were inside the eggshell.

"Do you imagine this is the whole world?" said the mother. "It stretches a long way on the other side of the garden, right into the parson's field; but I have never been as far as that! I suppose you are all here now?" and she got up. "No! I declare I have not got you all yet! The biggest egg is still there; how long is it going to last?" And then she settled herself on the nest again.

"Well, how are you getting on?" said an old duck who had come to pay her a visit.

"This one egg is taking such a long time," answered the sitting duck. "The shell will not crack; but now you must look at the others; they are the finest ducklings I have ever seen! They are all exactly like their father, the rascal! He never comes to see me."

"Let me look at the egg which won't crack," said the old duck. "You may be sure that it is a turkey's egg! I have been cheated like that once, and I had no end of trouble and worry with the creatures, for I may tell you that they are afraid of the water. I could not get them into it; I quacked and snapped at them, but it was no good. Let me see the egg! Yes, it is a turkey's egg! You just leave it alone and teach the other children to swim."

"I will sit on it a little longer. I have sat so long already that I may as well go on till the Midsummer Fair comes round."

"Please yourself," said the old duck, and she went away.

At last the big egg cracked. "Cheep, cheep!" said the young one and tumbled out; how big and ugly he was! The duck looked at him.

"That is a monstrous big duckling," she said. "None of the others looked like that. Can he be a turkey chick? Well, we shall soon find that out; into the water he shall go, if I have to kick him in myself."

Next day was gloriously fine, and the sun shone on all the green dock leaves. The mother duck with her whole family went down to the moat.

Splash, into the water she sprang. "Quack, quack!" she said, and one duckling plumped in after the other. The water dashed over their heads, but they came up again and floated beautifully; their legs went of themselves, and they were all there; even the big ugly gray one swam about with them.

"No, that is no turkey," she said; "see how beautifully he uses his legs and how erect he holds himself; he is my own chick! After all, he is not so bad when you come to look at him properly. Quack, quack! Now come with me and I will take you into the world, and introduce you to the duckyard; but keep close to me all the time, so that no one may tread upon you, and beware of the cat!"

Then they went into the duckyard. There was a fearful uproar going on, for two broods were fighting for the head of an eel, and in the end the cat captured it.

"That's how things go in this world," said the

mother duck, and she licked her bill for she wanted the eel's head herself.

"Use your legs," said she; "mind you quack properly, and bend your necks to the old duck over there! She is the grandest of them all; she has Spanish blood in her veins and that accounts for her size, and, do you see? she has a red rag round her leg; that is a wonderfully fine thing, and the most extraordinary mark of distinction any duck can have. It shows clearly that she is not to be parted with, and that she is worthy of recognition both by beasts and men! Quack now! Don't turn your toes in; a well-brought-up duckling keeps his legs wide apart just like father and mother; that's it, now bend your necks, and say quack!"

They did as they were bid, but the other ducks round about looked at them and said, quite loud: "Just look there! Now we are to have that tribe! Just as if there were not enough of us already; and, oh, dear! how ugly that duckling is; we won't stand him!" And a duck flew at him at once and bit him in the neck.

"Let him be," said the mother; "he is doing no harm."

"Very likely not, but he is so ungainly and queer," said the biter; "he must be whacked."

"They are handsome children mother has," said the old duck with the rag round her leg; "all good-looking except this one, and he is not a good specimen; it's a pity you can't make him over again."

"That can't be done, your grace," said the mother

duck; "he is not handsome, but he is a thoroughly good creature, and he swims as beautifully as any of the others; nay, I think I might venture even to add that I think he will improve as he goes on, or perhaps in time he may grow smaller! He was too long in the egg, and so he has not come out with a very good figure." And then she patted his neck and stroked him down. "Besides he is a drake," said she; "so it does not matter so much. I believe he will be very strong, and I don't doubt but he will make his way in the world."

"The other ducklings are very pretty," said the old duck. "Now make yourselves quite at home, and if you find the head of an eel you may bring it to me!"

After that they felt quite at home. But the poor duckling which had been the last to come out of the shell, and who was so ugly, was bitten, pushed about, and made fun of both by the ducks and the hens. "He is too big," they all said; and the turkey-cock, who was born with his spurs on, and therefore thought himself quite an emperor, puffed himself up like a vessel in full sail, made for him, and gobbled and gobbled till he became quite red in the face. The poor duckling was at his wit's end, and did not know which way to turn; he was in despair because he was so ugly, and the butt of the whole duckyard.

So the first day passed, and afterwards matters grew worse and worse. The poor duckling was chased and hustled by all of them; even his brothers

and sisters ill-used him; and they were always saying, "If only the cat would get hold of you, you hideous object!"

Even his mother said, "I wish to goodness you were miles away." The ducks bit him, the hens pecked him, and the girl who fed them kicked him aside.

Then he ran off and flew right over the hedge, where the little birds flew up into the air in a fright.

"That is because I am so ugly," thought the poor duckling, shutting his eyes, but he ran on all the same. Then he came to a great marsh where the wild ducks lived; he was so tired and miserable that he stayed there the whole night.

In the morning the wild ducks flew up to inspect their new comrade.

"What sort of a creature are you?" they inquired, as the duckling turned from side to side and greeted them as well as he could. "You are frightfully ugly," said the wild ducks; "but that does not matter to us, so long as you do not marry into our family!" Poor fellow! he had no thought of marriage; all he wanted was permission to lie among the rushes, and drink a little of the marsh water.

He stayed there two whole days; then two wild geese came, or rather two wild ganders. They were not long out of the shell, and therefore rather pert.

"I say, comrade," they said, "you are so ugly that we have taken quite a fancy to you; will you join us and be a bird of passage? There is another marsh close by, and there are some charming wild geese

183

there, all sweet young ladies who can say quack! You are ugly enough to make your fortune among them." Just at that moment, bang! bang! was heard up above, and both wild geese fell dead among the reeds, and the water turned blood red. Bang! bang! went the guns, and whole flocks of wild geese flew up from the rushes and the shot peppered among them again.

There was a grand shooting party, and the sportsmen lay hidden round the marsh; some even sat on the branches of the trees which overhung the water; the blue smoke rose like clouds among the dark trees and swept over the pool.

The water-dogs wandered about in the swamp, splash! splash! The rushes and reeds bent beneath their tread on all sides. It was terribly alarming to the poor duckling. He twisted his head round to get it under his wing and just at that moment a frightful, big dog appeared close beside him; his tongue hung right out of his mouth and his eyes glared wickedly. He opened his great chasm of a mouth close to the duckling, showed his sharp teeth — and — splash — went on without touching him.

"Oh, thank Heaven!" sighed the duckling, "I am so ugly that even the dog won't bite me!"

Then he lay quite still while the shot whistled among the bushes, and bang after bang rent the air. It only became quiet late in the day, but even then the poor duckling did not dare to get up; he waited several hours more before he looked about and then he hurried away from the marsh as fast as he could.

184

He ran across fields and meadows, and there was such a wind that he had hard work to make his way.

Towards night he reached a poor little cottage; it was such a miserable hovel that it could not make up its mind which way to fall even, and so it remained standing. The wind whistled so fiercely round the duckling that he had to sit on his tail to resist it, and it blew harder and harder; then he saw that the door had fallen off one hinge and hung so crookedly that he could creep into the house through the crack and by this means he made his way into the room. An old woman lived there with her cat and her hen. The cat, which she called "Sonnie," could arch his back, purr, and give off electric sparks, that is to say if you stroked his fur the wrong way. The hen had quite tiny short legs and so she was called "Chuckie-lowlegs." She laid good eggs, and the old woman was as fond of her as if she had been her own child.

In the morning the strange duckling was discovered immediately, and the cat began to purr and the hen to cluck.

"What on earth is that!" said the old woman looking round, but her sight was not good and she thought the duckling was a fat duck which had escaped. "This is a capital find," said she; "now I shall have duck's eggs if only it is not a drake! We must find out about that!"

So she took the duckling on trial for three weeks, but no eggs made their appearance. The cat was the master of the house and the hen the mistress, and they always spoke of "we and the world," for they thought that they represented the half of the world, and that quite the better half.

The duckling thought there might be two opinions on the subject, but the cat would not hear of it.

"Can you lay eggs?" the hen asked.

"No!"

"Will you have the goodness to hold your tongue then!"

And the cat said, "Can you arch your back, purr, or give off sparks?"

"No."

"Then you had better keep your opinions to yourself when people of sense are speaking!"

The duckling sat in the corner nursing his ill-humor; then he began to think of the fresh air and the sunshine; an uncontrollable longing seized him to float on the water, and at last he could not help telling the hen about it.

"What on earth possesses you?" she asked; "you have nothing to do; that is why you get these freaks into your head. Lay some eggs or take to purring, and you will get over it."

"But it is so delicious to float on the water," said the duckling; "so delicious to feel it rushing over your head when you dive to the bottom."

"That would be a fine amusement," said the hen. "I think you have gone mad. Ask the cat about it; he is the wisest creature I know; ask him if he is fond of floating on the water or diving under it. I say nothing about myself. Ask our mistress your-

self, the old woman; there is no one in the world cleverer than she is. Do you suppose she has any desire to float on the water, or to duck underneath it?"

"You do not understand me," said the duckling.

"Well, if we don't understand you, who should? I suppose you don't consider yourself cleverer than the cat or the old woman, not to mention me. Don't make a fool of yourself, child, and thank your stars for all the good we have done you! Have you not lived in this warm room, and in such society that you might have learned something? But you are an idiot, and there is no pleasure in associating with you. You may believe me I mean you well, I tell you home truths, and there is no surer way than that of knowing who are one's friends. You just see about laying some eggs, or learn to purr, or to emit sparks."

"I think I will go out into the wide world," said the duckling.

"Oh, do so by all means," said the hen.

So away went the duckling. He floated on the water and ducked underneath it, but he was looked askance at by every living creature for his ugliness. Now the autumn came on, the leaves in the woods turned yellow and brown; the wind took hold of them, and they danced about. The sky looked very cold, and the clouds hung heavy with snow and hail. A raven stood on the fence and croaked Caw! Caw! from sheer cold; it made one shiver only to think of it; the poor duckling certainly was in a bad case.

One evening, the sun was just setting in wintry splendor when a flock of beautiful large birds appeared out of the bushes; the duckling had never seen anything so beautiful. They were dazzlingly white with long waving necks; they were swans, and uttering a peculiar cry they spread out their magnificent broad wings and flew away from the cold regions to warmer lands and open seas. They mounted so high, so very high, and the ugly little duckling became strangely uneasy; he circled round and round in the water like a wheel, craning his neck up into the air after them. Then he uttered a shriek so piercing and so strange that he was quite frightened by it himself. Oh, he could not forget those beautiful birds, those happy birds, and as soon as they were out of sight he ducked right down to the bottom, and when he came up again he was quite beside himself. He did not know what the birds were, or whither they flew, but all the same he was more drawn towards them than he had ever been by any creatures before. He did not envy them in the least. How could it occur to him even to wish to be such a marvel of beauty? He would have been thankful if only the ducks would have tolerated him among them — the poor ugly creature!

The winter was so bitterly cold that the duckling was obliged to swim about in the water to keep it from freezing, but every night the hole in which he swam got smaller and smaller. Then it froze so hard that the surface ice cracked, and the duckling had to use his legs all the time, so that the ice should not close in round him; at last he was so weary that he could move no more, and he was frozen fast into the ice.

Early in the morning a peasant came along and saw him; he went out onto the ice and hammered a hole in it with his heavy wooden shoe, and carried the duckling home to his wife. There it soon revived. The children wanted to play with it, but the duckling thought they were going to ill-use him, and rushed in his fright into the milk pan, and the milk spurted out all over the room. The woman shrieked and threw up her hands. Then it flew into the butter cask, and down into the meal tub and out again. Just imagine what it looked like by this time! The woman screamed and tried to hit it with the tongs, and the children tumbled over one another in trying to catch it, and they screamed with laughter. By good luck the door stood open, and the duckling flew out among the bushes and the new-fallen snow, and it lay there thoroughly exhausted.

But it would be too sad to mention all the privation and misery it had to go through during that hard winter. When the sun began to shine warmly again, the duckling was in the marsh, lying among the rushes; the larks were singing and the beautiful spring had come.

Then all at once it raised its wings and they flapped with much greater strength than before, and bore him off vigorously. Before he knew where he was, he found himself in a large garden where the apple trees were in full blossom, and the air was scented with lilacs, the long branches of which overhung the indented shores of the lake. Oh! the spring freshness was so delicious!

Just in front of him he saw three beautiful white swans advancing towards him from a thicket; with rustling feathers they swam lightly over the water. The duckling recognized the majestic birds, and he was overcome by a strange melancholy.

"I will fly to them, the royal birds, and they will hack me to pieces, because I, who am so ugly, venture to approach them! But it won't matter; better be killed by them than be snapped at by the ducks, pecked by the hens, or spurned by the henwife, or suffer so much misery in the winter."

So he flew into the water and swam towards the stately swans; they saw him and darted towards him with ruffled feathers.

"Kill me, oh, kill me!" said the poor creature, and bowing his head towards the water he awaited his death. But what did he see reflected in the transparent water?

He saw below him his own image, but he was no longer a clumsy dark gray bird, ugly and ungainly. He was himself a swan! It does not matter in the least having been born in a duckyard, if only you come out of a swan's egg!

He felt quite glad of all the misery and tribulation he had gone through; he was the better able to appreciate his good fortune now, and all the beauty which greeted him. The big swans swam

round and round him, and stroked him with their bills.

Some little children came into the garden with corn and pieces of bread, which they threw into the water; and the smallest one cried out: "There is a new one!" The other children shouted with joy, "Yes, a new one has come!" And they clapped their hands and danced about, running after their father and mother. They threw the bread into the water, and one and all said that the new one was the prettiest; he was so young and handsome. And the old swans bent their heads and did homage before him.

He felt quite shy, and hid his head under his wing; he did not know what to think; he was so very happy, but not at all proud; a good heart never becomes proud. He thought of how he had been pursued and scorned, and now he heard them all say that he was the most beautiful of all beautiful birds. The lilacs bent their boughs right down into the water before him, and the bright sun was warm and cheering, and he rustled his feathers and raised his slender neck aloft, saying with exultation in his heart: "I never dreamt of so much happiness when I was the Ugly Duckling!"

HANS CHRISTIAN ANDERSEN

CDEFGHIJ—R—73210/6987

PIPER BOOKS